BRICKS WITHOUT STRAW

by

Ryder and Heather Rogers

LIFE-CHANGING BOOKS

A catalogue record of this book is available from the
British Library

ISBN 0-9530487-1-3

Copyright © 2000 Ryder and Heather Rogers.

All rights reserved. No part of this publication may be reproduced or transmitted in any form or by any means, electronic or mechanical, including photocopying, recording or any information storage and retrieval system, without either the prior permission in writing from the authors or a licence permitting restricted copying. In the United Kingdom such licenses are issued by the Copyright Licensing Agency, 33-35 Alfred Place, London WC1E 7DP.

The rights of Ryder and Heather Rogers to be identified as the joint authors of this work has been asserted by them in accordance with the Copyright, Designs and Patents Act 1988.

First Published March 2000 by
Life-Changing Books
48 The Crescent
Kettering.   NN15 7HW
UK

Printed by Creeds the Printers, Broadoak, Bridport DT6 5NL

FOREWORD

Lots of people tell stories but not everyone has a story to tell! This book is not just a very interesting account of the life of a Christian church planter in Bedfordshire but is a story that deserves to be heard and listened to by others.

I visited the church at Bramingham in all three of its phases. I remember speaking to a small group of Christians in Ryder and Heather's home. I remember visiting a builders' A-frame show house to see the fledgling congregation develop and I remember standing inside a complete church building and being amazed at how far things had come in a relatively short space of time.

This books records the struggles, pains and joys of gathering together a few people to pray and to plan to be salt and light in the local community. It's a story of how they experienced success and failure, great advances and frustrating setbacks .... and all the time, faithfully moving forward in the things of God.

This book will commend itself to many of us because there is a complete absence of trite and superficial suggestions. One is constantly made aware of the enormous hard work which is represented here. Ryder built a church and a church building. much of the work was done with his own hands! This is a story not just of hard work but of hope that, in the relatively unlikely setting of a building in the shadow of Sainsbury's, a group of God's people can begin the process of sharing its life with those in the community around.

If our nation is to won to Christ, it will probably happen as ordinary people do extraordinary things. It will probably happen as ordinary Christians live out their lives in what seems at first sight to be a relatively unspectacular way. However, it can have spectacular results.

May you find the ideas and the journey of faith described in this book stimulating and encouraging and may church planters everywhere draw from its truths and find their own success as they follow God's purposes for their lives.

Stephen Gaukroger

DEDICATION

This book is dedicated to the glory of our Lord Jesus,
who is the story;
to the many 'bricks' that made and make up
Bramingham Park Church;
and to our longsuffering daughters, Dawn and Rachel,
for all they put up with from such mad parents.

CONTENTS

	Introduction	7
ch 1.	Foundations	9
ch 2.	Footings	17
ch 3.	Obstructions	29
ch 4.	Basic Structures	41
ch 5.	Bricks and bits	53
ch 6.	Building up	68
ch 7.	Fittings that don't always fit	83
ch 8.	Windows and doors	92
ch 9.	Power Points	101
ch 10.	Extension Work	108
ch 11.	Extension work (continued)	118
ch 12.	An Inspector calls	125
ch 13.	Topping Off	132
ch 14.	Epilogue	141
	Appendices	143
	Study Guide	176

Introduction

How do you start a church from nothing with just yourself, your wife, two teenage daughters and a crossbreed dog called 'Saint'?

An Association of churches had called us to test the viability of a church on a new housing estate on the north east of Luton in Bedfordshire. Ten families a week were arriving and moving into houses where the plaster was still drying.

With money from the sale of an old redundant church they bought us a house and, though they continued to keep a prayerful interest in what we did, basically like on November 5th they lit the blue touch-paper... and waited for the fireworks to begin.

Most new churches are started with a nucleus, like a house group, from a mother church. That sort of way of starting a church is called a 'strawberry' plant - because of all the runners the mother church sends out.

Some new churches begin with a team that is sent into an new area, and by default that team becomes the base and pattern for a future fellowship.

But we were on our own.

Technically we were called, by those who classify and analyse these things, 'Pioneer Church Planters'.

In practical terms, for us, it meant freedom.

With no-one breathing down our necks, we were able to go back to first principles like asking basic questions such as 'Where does church work all begin?', 'What is a church anyway?', 'What's involved in being a church?', 'What do we mean by leadership?'.

With this liberation that we were given we were prayerfully able to challenge the preconceptions and structures that we and others followed, and in many ways be mould breakers.

Some twenty three years beforehand, from separate parts of the UK, we had both felt God calling us to train for different sorts of Christian service at London Bible College - which was nicknamed by some 'London Bridal College'. It will be no surprise then to learn that it was there that I met the young lady who was to become my future wife and fellow worker.

At LBC I had been trained in a 'one-man-ministry mould' that during the course of my pastoral ministry I had come to question.

However, the 'one-man' model that I had been given so many years earlier, in some ways became a good preparation for the heady and at times lonely experience of starting a church from zero.

I discovered in the first days of church planting that having had to be a sort of 'Do it All' person in previous churches did have some benefit to it after all!

- o O o -

In Egypt God's ancient people the Jews were being forced to build something really big for the Pharaoh-King.

At one period Moses, the adopted grandson of the King, after discovering his Jewish roots, turned up to help the Hebrews' cause. But rather than making life better things went from bad to worse. In desperation the people had to call out to God for help because, after Moses' intervention, their task masters forced them to build without some of the very basic components that would make their life and work easier. The order went out that they had to make 'bricks without straw'.

That was tough! And that's a bit like what it felt for us. I don't want to push the illustration too far because the Israelites had to build without straw as a judgement, whereas for us it was just a matter of difficulty and not a punishment! But, whatever the cause, just like them we were having to build something without many of the commonly accepted essentials that we had come to rely on over the previous years that we had been working. Because of this the task of 'building a church' was just like making 'bricks without straw'.

So, this is the story of our family adventuring with God and seeing Him come up trumps again and again, as 'the uncertain' (that's us) moved into 'the unknown' (that is pioneer church planting) where 'the Unpredictable' (that's God) helped us to experience 'the unexpected'.

If that hasn't put you off - read on ....

Chapter 1

Foundations

'O God, I think I'm going potty.'

Not exactly the most promising start for someone who is going to start a new church. The fact that God already had this up His sleeve for us (the beginning and building of a church) didn't figure in our calculations at all.

All I knew was this. As my wife and I were reading our Bible bit for the day at the breakfast table, a verse had leapt out at me. And I couldn't make head nor tail of it.

Well, what would you make out of 'I will bring them out of Egypt into Gilead and Lebanon, and there will not be room enough for them'?

But there it was, all sort of shiny in Zechariah 10:10.

When I told Heather how I thought this verse might be special, always the encourager, she said 'Then it must mean something'. But what it was we couldn't imagine!

Being the busy pastor of a large Baptist Church in Devon I hurriedly went off into my study to plan another full day, irreverently saying to God about that verse, 'Forget it.'

I did, but He didn't, as He had cause to remind me some time later.

- o O o -

Meanwhile 200 miles away another Baptist minister was walking through the middle of a cornfield talking to one of his church leaders.

They had heard that the 300 acre farm where they were now standing would be turned into Luton's premier housing estate for some 10,000 people.

'One of these days there is going to be a church here.' he said.

Together in prayer, surrounded by corn, they sowed a different sort of seed into that field that day - a seed of faith. And so by that simple act a church was planted.

- o O o -

At the same time as this praying and faith planting was going on, another piece in God's plan was clicking into place.

Some nine months before these events were about to come together, the Churches in the Torbay area had got involved in the visit of Billy Graham for Mission England. Despite a journey of 150 miles up country they had 'coach-ed' 1000's of people to Bristol. They had got so excited by all that happened that they decided to have a united 'follow-up' mission to the Torbay area nine months later. A number of evangelists were invited to speak at the various supporting churches as part of this mission.

So, at about the same period as people were praying over that 'church in the cornfield' in Luton, we, in the fishing port of Brixham, had a well know Spring Harvest speaker and evangelist - Ian Coffey - come to our church.

After he had spoken at our evening service, we went down onto the Quayside to hold our usual summer 'Open Air' service. There, by a replica of the Golden Hind, our church, with members from other churches in Brixham, regularly shared our faith with the 'suntan-oiled, chip-eating, sea-breeze-inhaling' holiday makers who needed to hear about Jesus.

I loved the cut and thrust way of sharing our faith - which at times could be unpredictable when some 'well-oiled' (not with tanning oil but beer and spirits) holiday makers asked questions, shouted comments and expressed objections to what we were saying.

When we had finished and were packing up to go home, Ian put his hand on my shoulder and said with a grin 'Brother, you're really a 'fisherman', your gift is evangelism.'

Over the next weeks it seemed as though there was a plot afoot as one holiday visitor after another would confide to me after the church services 'You won't be here much longer.' It felt a bit like Elisha being told that his master would soon be taken from him. Was God saying it was time to bring my will up to date or what?

Then back it came again, like the toothache that disappears when you visit the dentist only to return when you get home...THAT verse from Zechariah again...O no!

'Lord, It's your verse, not mine, what on earth does it mean?' I pleaded, fearing my sanity - or what little was left of it.

'What do the words mean?' whispered a little voice echoing my good old Bible College training.

'Gilead - a heap, a mound of witness', 'Lebanon - white' explained my Hebrew dictionary that always took me hours to decipher. 'That's a fat lot of good.' I thought. ' A real bundle of help that!'

As I wrestled with God's word through Zechariah I wondered whether I was becoming one of those church members who creep up on their minister and with a sideways look say 'The Lord has given me this word - about a bowl of soup with a funny bone in it.'

- o O o -

By now the Churches of Bedfordshire were thinking seriously and practically about that cornfield on the edge of Luton because already the bulldozers had moved on and started changing all those beautiful acres of farmland into roads, building sites, and show houses.

So far a large supermarket, owned by Sainsbury's, had been built in the centre, and 500 houses on the south west corner had been occupied.

By the supermarket, on what the local authorities called the community centre, a place had been allocated by the planners for a church. But what sort of church?

The denominations had been contacted though the local 'churches ecumenical committee', but after much discussion only the Baptists showed any interest in pioneering a church on the estate.

So the Bedfordshire Baptist Association, getting the green light from everybody, began by asking itself, ' Where do we start?' and 'Should a church property be built on the available land or a church planter be housed on the estate to start the work?'

The latter view prevailed.

- o O o -

A puzzled expression etched itself on my weary head. 'White' - my hair will be!' 'A mound'? - more like a burden!' I sighed. Then a thought surfaced.

Between Brixham and Broadsands was an area where some of our members lived called White Rock. Was that it? Was that what God was saying - plant a Church there?'

Strange how one thing can lead to another, one idea trigger another.

In this way the seed thought of Church Planting was sown in my heart.

However it wasn't to be as I thought, well, not at White Rock anyway.

After a bit more prayer and heart searching I 'phoned Ron Cowley, our Area Superintendent (our sort of 'Baptist bishop'), and told him how I was feeling and how I really wanted to get back to telling people about Jesus - to be more of a 'fisherman' (like Ian had said) rather than a 'vet' for the sheep in the church. That was a bit of a change from the times Heather had 'phoned him to say 'He wants to be a dustman again!' - my last resort when exasperated with the problems of church diplomacy.

'What are the possibilities of Church Planting?' I ventured in my conversation with him.

With that question in mind he went to Baptist Church House to talk with his colleagues, only to find one of them saying before he could ask, 'We are looking for someone to start a church on a new estate in Bedfordshire.'

Isn't God's timing perfect!

- o O o -

An enthusiastic Arthur Glinn (the minister who had stood in the cornfield all those months ago) showed me round the development enthusiastically waving arms here and there like a windmill as he explained 'shops will be here... a school there...more houses in that field...that's the Sales Information Office...let's look at Sainsbury's....' and so on.

My mind was in a whirl; but at its centre was emerging, like a rock around which a whirlpool forms, the exciting possibility that 'This' was 'It'.

Confirmation came in three ways.

First, the Beds. Baptist Association, after a relaxed interview, gave our family an invitation to 'test the viability of a church on the estate' over the next 5 years. Whilst we were there the Home Mission department of the Baptist Union said it they would financially sponsor us (so we had no need to find a job to keep us fed and clothed!).

Later one of the executive of the Beds. Association sent us a personal letter saying that all the prerequisites which he had jotted down before that meeting he had been able to tick off and, he said. he was sure that this was God's will for us.

Second, David Coffey (Ian's brother), who was at that time senior minister at Upton Vale, Torquay, and a respected friend to talk things over with said, 'I believe this is of God. Go for it.'

And thirdly - guess. Along with the unexpected realisation that the passage that the Lord had used to call me into the ministry 20 years earlier in Jeremiah 1 verses 4-10 which actually ends 'I send you ....to build and to plant.', would you believe it, THAT verse came back? Yes, Zechariah 10:10, 'to Gilead and Lebanon....' And still no explanation.

So after prayerfully putting all the bits together we agreed to leave sunny Brixham and move up to Luton and see what could be done.

- o O o -

The next three months were hectic. They included continuing and concluding a busy pastorate in a seaside town in the summer, packing for four (with over 1000 books), driving up to Luton to see to the girls' education in Luton (one was 16 and the other 14), a house to be bought on the estate where we would be working, saying goodbye to everyone in Brixham .... phew! All that was a story in itself.

- o O o -

On the evening of August 27th 1985 we arrived in Luton.

Tired and exhausted we struggled to lift out the back of our estate car a doped dog who, refusing to sleep despite the sedative the vet had given him, had yelped most of the way. He was so 'under the influence' however that he couldn't walk straight. In fact at one comfort stop on the way when he tried to cock his leg up he simply fell flat on face.

Three days later, when we found our Apples of Gold calendar that was hidden in all the muddle of the things to be unpacked (some of which never got done before we left some 8 years later!), it said for August 27th 'My presence shall go with thee, and I will give thee rest.' Exodus 33:14. That was an encouragement.

But as the day got nearer for our official 'Induction Service' that the authorities and local churches wanted to put on, which to our minds was really a welcome time, all sorts of questions and doubts started to surface.

Questions, that I asked with a mischievous grin, like 'How can my wife and I be inducted to 'the initial pastorate of Bramingham Park Church' when there is no church in existence to pastor?'

But more serious were the doubts that were starting to surface like a ghoul out of the misty marshes. Questions about whether we really were doing the right thing anyway.

It got to the point when I was almost panicking over the thought of answering the question that Area Superintendents ask during an induction service: 'Do you believe you are truly called of God to this work?' Sneaky voices were saying 'You're not, are you?'

The day before it was all to happen, as I was praying more or less constantly that prayer of faith 'HELP', a bit from the Bible popped into my head 'Go up the mountain.'

What mountain? I asked myself. There are no mountains in Luton. This wasn't Nepal or Switzerland. The only bump on the horizon was a hillock called Warden Hill.

To hear is to obey, especially when you are desperate. So, that night found me on top of Warden Hill surveying the twinkling lights of our estate that nestled below it.

Now what? 'Lord I need to hear from you....please.'

Silence....

So I prayed for Bramingham Park. Just about everything I could think of - the people, the problems, the possibilities. I sang some songs of praise as I worshipped the Lord. 'Please Lord, speak.' I started to groan.

Silence....

And then eventually, silence from me. I'd run out of things to say. And was getting cold.

Suddenly a bright light filled the sky. My heart thumped with excitement. 'An angel with God's message.' I thought. I'd heard how God had done that for others. Was he sending one to little me?

'That's not fair, God.' I moaned as the light above me droned overhead and I realised it was a night flight returning with some holiday makers from Corfu to Luton Airport.

I realised it was a night flight returning .... from Corfu

It was now 3.00am, I was cold, and wanted to go to bed. Again I waited.

'The work is mine.' a voice whispered in the dark, 'I am sending you to release the captives.'

'Thank you Lord.' I smiled. 'Thank you.' I shouted. Then less noisily I whispered, 'Now I can get some sleep.'

- o O o -

One Friday evening, a number of weeks later, because the girls were missing the sea, we went down to Dorset to visit my Mum, who lived a mere 200 yards from the beach.

We left her home as late as possible on Saturday evening to get the best out of our time by the sea, and arrived in Luton just before midnight.

The next morning, as I was praying and going over what to say at the Sunday afternoon service that we had started in our front room, surreptitiously like a spectre looming, THAT verse sneaked up and over me again.

'I will bring you out of Egypt into Gilead and Lebanon, and there will not be room enough for you.'

Oh no, not again. 'Lord, it doesn't make sense - a mound, that's white. Either tell me what it means or ....'

'Get up, and look.' said that voice that seemed to come out of nowhere at the back of my mind.

As I looked out of the window of my upstairs room the sun shone over the houses and fields and seemed to spotlight the community plot where the pub, doctors and church were to be.

On the Friday when we went down to Dorset the contractors had moved on site to start the pub and its car park.

The earthmover had stripped away the clay topsoil and removed it, and had levelled the subsoil dumping it where the church would be built.

As the subsoil glistened in the sunlight - pure chalk - God said 'There it is - the MOUND of witness that is WHITE, and there will not be room enough for you.'

'Thank you Lord.' I breathed with a sigh of relief and with a whoop of excitement called out for Heather to come and have a look. Wow! What a prophecy and promise to build on! What a foundation for a Church!

Chapter 2
Footings

We would have probably died of fright if some fiery or spidery writing had slowly appeared on the piece of paper in front of us. Together, on one of our earliest days in our new house, Heather and I had knelt by our big sofa with a blank piece of paper in front of us and prayed 'Lord, it's your church. You write the agenda for us.'

Of course He didn't actually write anything (not literally that is), but He did take us at our word (He always does) and gradually over the weeks and months He uncovered bit by bit, step by step, His plans for us.

Sometimes Heather had what she called 'a hunch', and what I very spiritually call 'a word of knowledge or wisdom'. Sometimes God gave us a bit from the Bible. Sometimes it was, well, like a voice in the back of our mind saying 'That's what I want.' We had to be open to all the means that God wanted to use - even angels (I was still waiting for one).

So there I was praying and wondering. My question was: How, and where, do you start a church from nothing, with just you, your wife, two teenage daughters, and a crossbreed dog called 'Saint' (well, a name like that gave him something to aspire to in a clergy house, especially as his previous name had been 'Tramp')?

In fact it all started quite naturally.

As our inter-continental removal lorry pulled up outside the house that the Bedfordshire Baptist Association had bought (partly with the proceeds from the sale of a nearby chapel and partly with a mortgage) the neighbours stared at the large writing that announced to everyone where we had come from 'Brixham-TORQUAY'.

'What are you doing coming up here?' people asked 'We're trying to get down there!'

Not wanting to blow my cover (well, you know what people think of clergymen. Just sit in a railway carriage with a clerical collar on and see how it empties or goes embarrassingly and unnaturally quiet) so I said 'It's my job' or 'The boss sent me up here.' People nodded knowingly. Much of the estate was in transition due to work.

It wasn't until some weeks later, when they had seen me in my shorts, watched me struggling with the garden of a new house just as they had, had been helped to get the gas boiler going by one of them, and they had discovered that I was quite normal, not until then did I let it out that I was here to start the church for the estate.

So how did it all start?

Soon after we arrived an inquisitive 5 year old from across the road wandered over to bombard us with questions and regale us with his knowledge of anything we wanted to know about the estate.

When Heather asked him what he wanted to be when he grew up he said 'A Boss'. David, who is still with the church, and much the same, quite happily knocked on any doors to borrow whatever we needed. This gave us a golden opportunity to chat with the 'loaners' when we took things back. A bit like Jesus when he was tired and thirsty and got into conversation with someone who helped him.

Then God used our girls.

We were concerned about our two teenage daughters with their Deb'nshr accents in the foreign culture of Luton, but a teenage girl next door took them to the fair on our second day and introduced them to some of her friends.

While the girls were at the fair I was looking for something in the garage when a young mum appeared. 'Hello.' she ventured 'Are you the new vicar?'

'Sort of.' I replied, worried about my street cred.

'I'm Lisa. My husband and two girls have heard about you. We go to the nearest Baptist Church and were told about you coming here. We live on this estate.'

The next day I was again in the garage (looking for something else in all the chaos of those tea-chests and boxes) when a be-hatted matronly lady appeared.

'I'm Dorothy Mandrak.' she announced, a bit like Margaret Rutherford. 'I live in the Help the Aged complex at the top of this road. I've heard that you are starting a church on this estate.

It needs it. I'm a member of the Methodist Church, but it's a long way to walk there with my bad legs.'

We weren't supposed to have started officially until our formal welcome and Induction, and that was still over a month ahead.

However, as in most church planting set-ups the rules rarely seem to apply.

God was already giving opportunities and forging links. After all when we had prayed by our sofa we had said it was to be His agenda!

I was champing at the bit to get going. This was exciting. So I walked the estate praying and jotting down the names of the roads on flip cards, noting all the houses still unoccupied or for sale.

There were 849 occupied and 164 uninhabited with 2000 still to go.

- o O o -

Denominations tend to have preset formulae.

Church planting makes you question everything, especially the traditions and assumptions that the establishment has. Constantly I asked myself and others when faced with church terminology and practice 'What does that mean? Why do church people do that? What does the Bible have to say about this and that?'

Despite my cheeky questioning of our official welcome being billed as an 'Induction to an Initial Pastorate' when there was no church to pastor?' in fact by the time that meeting arrived we were some way down the road to starting the church.

A fortnight after arriving we had a coffee evening with six interested people. and then on the Sunday before our Induction we invited people to a tea which was unexpectedly followed by an informal service after one of the children asked a pertinent (not impertinent) question.

On that first Sunday Lisa and David came with their two girls, their friends Andrew and Christine with their two girls, Dorothy (from the Help the Aged complex), Val and Hilary (a couple in their late 40's), John and Beverley (recently married and new to the estate), Titia (a youngish widow), Sue (really committed to another church but interested to see what was going on) and us four. Thirteen adults, two teenagers, and four children.

When we had finished explaining the answer to that question and had a song and a prayer we agreed to meet again in three weeks time. In the meanwhile we would all pray about whether God wanted us to be involved in this new work, and if we should start meeting together on a weekly basis.

On October 27th 1985 eleven of us prayerfully decided that we were ready to meet each Sunday and see where the Lord led us.

The next week, just 10 weeks after moving up from Devon, 14 adults, 4 children, and two teenagers squashed into our front room for a very informal family worship time - observed through the French windows by our most curious dog. Everyone joined in (even the dog at times) as we sang, prayed, shared interests, and looked at Matthew 16:18 in order to answer the question 'What do we mean by 'Church'? After holding hands and singing the prayer called 'The Grace' we tucked into tea together - something we were still doing right up until the Sunday we left eight years later.

- oOo -

By now I was out regularly pounding the patch, welcoming the 1½ new families that were arriving each day, as well as saying 'Hello' to those who had moved in before us.

Before long all the sales personnel and builders put aside their doubts about this funny little man who kept turning up as they got to know who I was. In the end they were telling me what houses would be occupied and the removal day for each family that would arrive.

Personal contact was so profitable. Years later people still remember the 'little man with a big grin' who welcomed them to their new home, and told them where the doctor, nearest Post Office, Chemist, only letter box, and open market on the next estate, could be found.

'Are you from the Residents' Association?' was the frequent question I was asked.

'No.' I would explain. ' By Sainsburys is the Community Patch where there's to be a health centre, pub, and church. I'm responsible for the church. I'm the ... (I remembered the look of fear when I'd said to a Sales Ladies at one of the many Show Houses on our estate 'I'm a minister' and she asked 'From which department?' thinking I was a Government Official!)...a sort of ... vicar.'

One of the things you learn in church planting is how the 'Church' has its own in-language. You have to learn to be normal in words and ideas and take nothing for granted.

The 'vicar' bit, opened the conversation up into 'What religion are you?'

'Christian.' was my right and proper answer (though Hospital computers, as I was later to discover, have data neither for that, nor the occupation - 'clergyman')

'What's that?' was the one in five response. And so I was in, both spiritually as well as literally. Many were the times I ended up in peoples' houses praying with them on my first visit. This was what I'd longed for. To get back to basics - talking to people about Jesus.

'Hello, I'm Ryder. I live over by the roundabout.... We're building a church....' I was almost saying it in my sleep. But it paid off.

- o O o -

'Can anyone come to your church? I'm, well... I'm ...er.... Catholic.' said the cheerful well dressed young lady accountant, as though that might stop her from coming to us.

'There is only one Christian family, and we want to express that.' I explained. 'As there will only be one church on this estate we simply want to be known as Christians. So it's open to everyone.'

'But my husband he can't come,' she stated quite firmly. 'he's a Buddhist....from Malaysia.'

'Jesus loves Buddhists.' I replied. 'He'd be delighted for him to come.' With this beginning a lasting friendship was struck up with Julie and her husband Wan.

Some months later Julie gave her heart fully to Jesus in our kitchen. Earlier occasional church attendance now became personal faith.

Wan at the time was the Deputy Manager of the Chiltern Crest Hotel. Later they were moved to Welwyn when he was promoted to be Manager there. Despite this they still travelled back for occasional services. Then he was promoted back to Luton to manage the other main Crest Hotel. They were delighted to be able to move back onto the estate, and we were thrilled to have them.

Then things at the hotel got difficult, so Wan applied for a job with the Stakis Hotel chain. God was doing all sorts of things in Wan's life at this time. He was amazed at the number of times God answered our prayers for him, and then how God answered his own stumbling prayers.

It all came to a head for him some weeks before he left for yet another new job, this time in Bristol. As we were singing 'Father God, I wonder how I managed to exist without the knowledge of your parenthood and your loving care.'[1] it was as he sang the words 'Now I am your son' that it happened. Something clicked into gear and he entered the family of Jesus Christ as he made the words his own.

How lovely to hear Wan share his testimony and then to serve both him and his wife with communion and then to lay hands on them both the week Wan left for Bristol.

'Father God.' has never been the same since.

- o O o -

John and Beverley were a recently married couple who had just moved into one of the 'one-bedroom matchboxes' on the development. They were a lovely Christian couple who were really excited about worshipping and working with us.

There were an number of good reasons we were glad to have them with us.

First they brought along John's parents and sister - the Kebles from Kensworth. Second, John was keen to help with the young people that were coming to our house. Thirdly, he was a Construction Engineer. Inquisitive young David who lived

---

(1). 'Father God' © Ian Smale Thankyou Music

opposite us, his dad was an architect in the Town Hall. So with these two to turn to we'd be alright for the start of the church building!

Last but not least, Beverley, who was a school teacher, wanted to help us with Rainbow Club.

Rainbow club began when some of the parents of our little group became concerned about a Halloween party arranged for their children at the local school. In its place and as a contrast we decided to have a party of our own. One to do with light not darkness.

We called the event a Rainbow Party.

Six children, two teenagers, and two adults came. The party was so enjoyed by the youngsters that they wanted another one - the next week! In this way Rainbow Club was born - a kid's club for those that came to the Sunday Family Worship, to have fun and look at the Bible.

That was the children sorted out.

To complement this time for the children a Monday evening time for prayer, looking at the Bible in greater depth, and sharing problems began for anyone who might be interested.

Gradually a family of God was forming in line with a word that God had given us early on - 'Be My Family.' We attempted to become this by celebrating every Sunday afternoon with all ages the joy of being one in Jesus.

Many churches have an identity crisis. They don't know who they are or what God wants them to be, so right at the beginning we asked the Lord what He had to say about us.

One Sunday evening, as we were starting up everything, while a small group of us were praying He gave us first a promise from Matthew 16:18 'I will build My church', then a prophecy 'Be My family'. With this he said 'You Be...I'll Build'.

Two things struck us about this.

First, He was to be in charge. The Lord said 'MY church', 'MY family'.

Second, we were to be a family - His Family - which led us into the idea of Sunday afternoon family celebrations every week for all ages together, with small groups meeting during the week to dig deeper into what God had for us.

We thought that this was a bit like Jesus. He majored on two aspects.

First he dealt with the crowd, a time where everyone came - all shapes, sizes, and ages - and he spoke in stories and got people involved - especially the children.

Then he spoke on a deeper level, often in small groups, with those who were interested to learn more.

- oOo -

Sometime within our first six months Heather had this, what she described as a 'hunch' about getting some of the neighbouring mums, who hadn't at that point made any commitments to Jesus, to come and look together into two books of the Bible - Jonah and Malachi!.

It was her hunch, so let her tell it to you.

- oOo -

'When you move to Luton you won't have a church to start with, so you will have plenty of spare time' said Lynn Green and Jean Raddon of C.W.C.I (Christian Womens Conventions International).

'Why not do some work on Bible Study Notes for K.Y.B. (their 'Know Your Bible' course).'

What had happened was that some years earlier our Young Wives group at Brixham had been fired with enthusiasm when visiting other groups in Torbay who were eagerly studying the Bible with K.Y.B notes. This caught on, and when we left Brixham over 100 ladies were studying the Scriptures using this method. This scheme, which had originated in Australia, was spreading like a bush fire to many areas of the U.K.

Now, when asked to write for them I felt pleased but daunted at the prospect.

Finding there was little prepared on the minor prophets, after prayer, I agreed to tackle Jonah and Malachi, and possibly later to attempt Haggai and Zechariah.

After our move I made a start.

At our Baptist Ministers' Wives conference in the September (one month after we had moved to Luton) I remember scribbling jottings between sessions, and soon I had prepared a rough plan and the first lesson.

When I sent this off I was told 'Before you go any further we must inform you that the material will need to be used by at least two pilot groups before it can be submitted for publishing.'

Pilot groups?

Within seconds an idea had formed. I am sure it was from God.

During the next few days I began finding my first pilot group.

I saw no point whatsoever in assembling a group of well-churched ladies (not that we had many at the time). I needed people who could spot jargon, the in-church phrases, the empty cliches and repetition. People who could help me make the studies life-related. So I asked various neighbours in, to help with the proof reading, having explained what I was doing.

Right from the start Ryder eagerly offered to run a creche for the pre-schoolers of those mothers who came.

Christine, Linda, Rita, and Liz, our neighbours, were the first ones to come, and while we studied the Bible Ryder played with the little ones.

This continued for many months - with picnics and social events thrown in. Even now the Tuesday group we hold in the church (complete with Ryder in the creche) is a development of that early pilot group.

When this first group was well under way I started a second pilot group composed of Lisa, Isobel, Caroline, and Sue - most of whom were at work during the day. This evening group highlighted other areas needing alteration, and ensured that the study book was not only of relevance to mothers with babies!

By the time I came to write some notes on Haggai and Zechariah (two other Old Testament prophets) I had the benefit of three pilot groups. A morning group of retired ladies - Eva, Millie, Marjorie and Ruth. This group makes me smile (even now) as I remember rocking with laughter at some of the comments that they made. Betty, Diane, Maureen, and another Christine all worked part or full time so we used to thrash out the manuscripts on a Tuesday afternoon. Then, finally, a group that never quite completed the course comprising of Hilary, Pauline, Jan, Anne, and Pat (all committed Christians who by then were attending Bramingham Park Church) who put me through my paces on grammar and punctuation and had a valuable contribution to make.

Unfortunately Haggai/Zechariah has not yet been published. However, looking back I can see that these pilot groups were instrumental in bringing many of those ladies to faith in Christ, bringing some back to Him, and enriching all of us as we studied the Bible together.'

- o O o -

You know what dogs are like. Ours was no exception. He might have had the name 'Saint' but he wasn't. Despite this, it's a fact that nose-to-nose-dogs bring face-to-face owners.

'Morning.' 'Morning.' 'Bit brisk today eh?'

Nose-to-nose dogs bring face-to-face owners

Sometimes real conversations could begin during 'walkies' times, though invariably they got cut short at the most important part by either a snarl that warned of an impending dog fight or a yank that said 'if you don't come now, I'll do it here.'

However over the years friendships did develop. Invitations to events given and accepted, and opportunities taken to talk about the problems of life and Jesus as a personal friend.

In fact, it was one of these dog owners that ended up screeding the church floor - even though his dog nipped me somewhere painful while we were talking about it in the Park! But the Bible does encourage us to help others to faith 'by all possible means.'

I can see it now throughout the country, readers everywhere ready to form the 'Dog-Walkers Evangelistic Programme' - Provide your own shin guards!!

- o O o -

It was great fun all squashed together in our house each Sunday, but something had to be done especially as Christmas loomed over the horizon.

There was only one property, apart from Sainsbury's entrance, that was in any way suitable, that was the Sales Information Office. This was a wooden A-frame structure owned by the building consortium, where clients in the early days used to be able to get details from the five construction firms about their different properties. No one used it now because people interested in buying something went directly to the show homes instead.

After negotiations with the head of the consortium we hired it for our first Christmas so as to have a Midnight Carol Service, and Christmas Day birthday celebration.

A thousand Birthday Cards for Jesus were delivered, one to each house, inviting people to come and join us. And we waited.

Some Christians from other churches came and supported our first 'public' effort. One church loaned us 100 chairs, which was great because that first Christmas Eve we had exactly 100 people squashed into the Sales Information Office (that most folk simply called 'The A-frame') to celebrate for the first time on the estate the coming of the King.

Christmas Eve became a real tradition for the locals. It was a welcoming non-threatening half hour.

People often came to us directly from the pub opposite, sometimes in colourful fancy dress. One chap whipped off his 'dog-collar' before leaving the pub for fear of being asked by someone about the service. Well, he would have been the only one in clerical garb - I certainly didn't wear the uniform.

Despite this, generally people were respectful at the midnight service, even if in our second year one young husband totally embarrassed his wife on their first visit to us. I had just explained that one of our members, a solicitor called Robin, would read to us the Christmas story when this young man overcome by his earlier Christmas celebrations slowly sank to the floor calling out 'Go for it Robin, go for it.'

Somewhat shamefacedly he apologised a few days later, but that was the opportunity to explain that God, in his love, accepts us as we are, and always forgives.

This started another good friendship, both with him and his family.

Beginning in the new year of 1986 we hired the A-frame for our regular Sunday afternoon services. Every week for the next four years (until we'd built our own place) we were seen lugging over chairs, musical instruments, Over Head Projector, crockery, Calor gas heater, songbooks etc., in fact everything we needed.

We celebrated the start of the new year in the A-frame, after tea, with our first communion.

Chapter 3

Obstructions

'Footings', mentioned in the previous chapter, aren't anything to do with what young people in love do with their feet under the table (that's footsy) but are the trenches dug out for the cement that forms the foundation of a building.

Many were the times when digging out those footings, or trenches for the drains on the church site, when we later started to build a building, that I jarred my wrist as with either spade or pickaxe I hit a lump of solid chalk or some other obstacle.

Often, during the process of the building going up, when people were cutting wood or nailing up plasterboard, a yell would echo around the place as someone cut or hit something that drew blood. TCP and Elastoplasts were always on tap.

Hitting something that shouldn't be there was an occupational hazard, Building is a risky business whether it's building a property or people.

That was true for Jesus. The first time he ventured to speak in his home church about building the kingdom of God they tried to push him over a cliff. The next week at Capernaum wasn't much better - as soon as he started to speak someone disrupted the service by screaming. But that's part of the package. Wherever the light shines the darkness gets shown up.

Church planting is not only hazardous it's a war of the worlds.

If you want to do something for God without difficulties or opposition, forget it. Jesus had problems. Who do we think we are that we should be let off so lightly?

I suppose our problems began even before we arrived. But let Heather tell you about this bit:

- o O o -

'During those early days we had many conflicting thoughts and emotions. At times we felt that we had done the work God had planned for us in Brixham and it was time for the church to have a new leader, with new vision and direction for the future.

Yet the supernatural 'vision' the Lord had given to Ryder for Brixham had not been fulfilled - which begs the question: 'Is the vision given to one person necessarily to be fulfilled during their ministry, or even their lifetime?' The record of Scripture and the experiences of others show that sometimes people see their vision fulfilled, but not always.

Compared with the exceptionally clear guidance we had received about going to our first church, and the clear (though different) directions to the second, this was most confusing. Some days the Bible, the advice of friends, and our own inner conscience said 'Stay'. Other days the verdict was 'Go'.

Was this because we were physically and emotionally drained and spiritually numb? At times I felt 'Am I so bad that God isn't speaking to me any more? Had we missed some vital clue? Had we listened to the voice of Satan? Were we being misled? Were our motives pure? Were we seeking God wholeheartedly?' These, and many other questions bombarded us.

And life had to go on. There were still the immediate needs and commitments.

In retrospect, I believe God was 'stretching' us.

The first 'call' had been crystal clear with a 100% invitation after we had prayed for this on the basis of a verse from Proverbs that promised 'Commit your ways to the Lord and your thoughts will be established'. We were very young and inexperienced (Ryder was only 23 at the time that he became pastor, simultaneously in charge of two churches - one with a long tradition in Tiverton town centre, and the other a small country chapel in nearby Ash Thomas). We needed a clear call.

The second 'call' had required a great deal of prayer and heart searching; and now the third possible move was a real challenge to our faith.

I believe that God was teaching us not to make assumptions. Just as the churches were different so the 'calls' and circumstances were different. This was a valuable lesson to learn for the future. God is a God of surprises. He is an innovator, the great Creator, and he needed to teach us lessons in growth and flexibility.

Running alongside these questions was a concern for our

daughters.

I knew very definitely that the Lord had their best interests in mind, and that he loved them every bit as much as he did us. But I had days when my faith was a little bit 'wobbly'. Would the change from a small country grammar school to a large comprehensive school and college in Luton be too much of a culture shock? How would they cope? Had they been too sheltered? How would this move effect their educational needs?

Though there were struggles and adjustments, I need not have worried. God answered all our prayers and provided for our girls. You ask them now!'

- o O o -

'It's us again.'

I felt that we had almost become school kids again the number of times we had presented ourselves at the school office, despite 14 year old Rachel's plea 'Don't make a fuss.'

In Brixham she had been set for 8 O'level G.C.E.'s and we had just discovered her new school had entered her for only one - Art!

We pushed this way, and that, bothered and badgered the staff until eight months later we had 'up-ed' the total to 4 O'levels. Eventually she left with 6 O'levels and 3 GCSE's.

We felt that this was one of the subtle oppositions we faced.

Alongside this was sickness.

It came in sort of waves (being sick generally does, but I don't mean that sort of being sick!)

For most of the first six months one, or more, of us was down at the doctors for something!

Six months later the next round hit us.

Both of our girls went down with a serious bout of chicken pox, but so did a number in our church family - which I suppose is an occupational hazard when everyone greets one another with a bear hug. 'Sharing' in our church meant not only telling what God had done but receiving what the others had got!!

'Sharing'... meant more than just telling what God had done but receiving what others had got!

This was followed by a wave of accidents.

One of our young teenagers, David, was rushed to hospital unconscious after being hit by a car on his way home from school. His leg was in traction having been broken in three places.

Paul, Rachel's boyfriend, broke his arm after coming off his bike.

Hilary's car was hit and its back axle broken by another car on the A6. This resulted in months off work with whiplash and vertigo problems.

Asif's car was damaged in an accident.

Our neighbour, little David's dad, also called David (isn't it confusing all these David-s) ended up in hospital with his leg also in traction after a football match (some football game!)

Then came waves of depression, first hitting this person, then that one.

What was going on?

When there was a wave of accidents with the babies and little children, the spiritual penny dropped.

As we prayed against the 'spiritual powers' that wanted to stop the growing influence of King Jesus, we were given a 'picture' like on D-Day when wave after wave of aircraft filled the sky - first the observer craft, then the fighter planes, then the bombers.

That was it. We were in a battle.

Of course, knowing we are in a battle doesn't stop the battle. So it wasn't surprising that by the end of 1987 I was rushed into hospital in an ambulance, blue lights flashing (it was exciting), with a suspected heart attack.

One of our newer members, Liz, who is an accident sister, and was always around when I turned up at the hospital to visit people was there to greet me as I arrived. 'We must stop meeting like this.' she grinned.

After a weekend, during which I was fitted up with silk stockings (to stop thrombosis, or so the doctor said), wired up to a heart monitor (which I unplugged to go to the toilet and caused a major panic because the staff thought they'd lost me, which they had - I was in the loo), and enduring various tests, I was sent home with a perfect bill of health.

Satan can counterfeit all sorts of things, even heart attacks, to serve his purposes.

He doesn't like being exposed, and even less being expelled. And that was what was going on.

When we take people as they are, there is a lot more openness and reality in becoming a Christian. And if we allow the Holy Spirit space to work in freeing people, a lot more of Satan's activity surfaces.

This happened for Rita, our neighbour and the first to give her life to Jesus. And it was Heather who helped her. So let her take over:

- o O o -

'I think the Lord wanted to teach me to be less dependant on Ryder. He certainly wanted me to grow, so he threw me in at the deep end.

We had become friendly with a family nearby, and the wife was part of the pilot group helping with the proof reading of the Jonah/Malachi notes.

One evening I called on her and we chatted over a coffee while we enjoyed the peace of their lovely self-built home.

As we talked about the difference Christ makes in a person's life, Rita admitted that though she had always believed in God to varying degrees she really wanted to welcome Jesus into her life. I explained what the Bible says, and how this can happen, and then prayed for Rita.

I then asked if she would like to pray, in her own words, asking God's forgiveness and inviting Christ to come into her life to be Saviour and King.

As she prayed she was gripped by fear and panic and felt the presence of 'something dark and evil' preventing her. She became very distressed.

There was no time to go looking for Ryder or read up some manual on deliverance. My mind flashed back to the Scriptures. I said to the evil presence 'Go, in the name of Jesus Christ. Jesus is Lord. Go, everything of darkness, and never come back.' I then prayed for the Holy Spirit to come on Rita and give protection and enable her to give her life to Christ.

The darkness lifted. She was freed.

Although she felt 'wobbly', the 'thing' went and the presence of Jesus came, and she was truly 'born again' into the family of God. During that night, and in the days that followed Rita knew the presence of Christ in some very special ways.

For example. That summer she went on a holiday to North Devon with a friend's church group. As she sat on her own, feeling lonely with an empty seat beside her at a full communion service and told the Lord how she felt, she became aware of a warm comforting arm around her shoulder. It was the Lord.

Another time, after a period of uncertainty, she heard the Lord say to her 'You shall rejoice.'

Another special occasion was when, after the Lord seemed to have left her for a while, she prayed for him to return and the room, and for some days following wherever she went, was filled with the strange fragrance of what she described as Lily of the Valley. It wasn't until later that she was shown the verse in Song of Songs 2:1 'I am the lily of the valley.'

- o O o -

Richard was three.

'Is he too old to be dedicated...or whatever you do?' asked his parents.

My reply was 'We bless children like Jesus, and we're never too old to get whatever the Lord wants to give.'

Some days later I was round at Liz (our nurse friend) and Ian's sipping tea as they put Michelle, who was 6½ and in Rainbow Club, and young Richard to bed. We could then talk about what was on offer in a 'Blessing Service'.

As I explained about the responsibilities of parents to 'bring up' their children 'in the knowledge and love of the Lord' I popped the question 'So tell me about your spiritual journey.'

Liz shared how she had given her life over to Jesus some years before, had let things slide, but was now on the way up.

Ian admitted he hadn't.

In the course of our conversations Ian mentioned how as a 16 year old he'd got involved with a group of spiritualists through a school friend who, by calling on 'spirit guides', practised automatic writing. This started him looking at all sorts of religions whilst also getting confirmed!

Later on, Ian's own words about his involvement with that group were, 'This left me severely damaged and scarred.'

As he was explaining all this, at that particular point the Holy Spirit gave me one of his nudges right in my stomach. But I kept quiet about it.

'Would you like to welcome Jesus into your life?' I asked Ian. 'Yes.' he replied.' He bowed his head, wrung his hands, huffed and puffed a bit, and said 'I can't seem to do it. Nothing's happening.'

'I think I know why. ' I ventured. 'You've got like a rope round you stopping you. Let me pray first, and then you welcome Jesus into your life as Lord.'

I simply prayed against what the occult had done in Ian's life. In the name of Jesus I broke the power of Satan, and gave freedom to Ian in Jesus' name so that he might be able to ask the Lord into his life.

I had hardly finished praying when, like a sudden birth, Ian broke down in front of the Lord, said sorry for all the things he'd done wrong, and welcomed Jesus into His life as Lord. I prayed for Ian to be filled with the Holy Spirit, and waited till he came.

Ian was free.

Later he shared this story when he and his wife were baptised together as believers. This was after Jesus met him dramatically on the M1 whilst driving to work in Milton Keynes. The Lord simply said to him 'OK, you've trusted me, now get baptised.'

You're never spiritually safe, not even on the motorway.

- o O o -

John was God's gift to us.

He was our worship leader, a 'proper' church organist and choirmaster yet humble enough to play our little Casio synthesizer in the Sales Information Office.

John was concerned about his dad who was seriously ill.

We were on a visit at John and Jan's house when the subject got round to sharing our faith with our families, and Heather said something about how important it is not only to pray for people, but with them.

We were having a time of prayer together when the 'phone rang. John looked up through his parted fingers as Jan said that it was his mother to say that his dad was critically ill.

Heather had one of those compelling 'hunches'. 'Go now, and look for the opportunity to talk with him about the Lord.' she said.

A sense of urgency gripped us as John left to drive across Luton. It was as though death wanted to get there first.

We prayed in the name of Jesus against the spirit of death. I stood by the window, arms stretched out as though holding back death until John's dad could respond to Jesus. I'd never done anything like that before, but God's Spirit seemed to compel us. We continued to pray like this for at least a couple of hours. Then the crisis looked, and felt, as though it must have passed.

God's moments are strange. Out of the agony of prayer and spiritual warfare we had got so close to the Lord. And as Jan was there, so taken up with Jesus and not wanting to leave, I gently laid my hands on her and thanked the Lord for his presence and help. For some reason I felt compelled to quietly pray 'Now give her a language of praise.'

Slowly, and beautifully, another language flowed from Jan's lips. In pain, praise.

The next morning John returned home radiating God's peace, having prayed with his father before he had died. Not only that, he found God's bonus as Jan told him her story.

Opposition is God's opportunity for outwitting Satan.

The next extra to all of this came some time later.

John and Jan had taken their two children to a holiday activity event run by the local authority in one of the town's parks.

While they waited in the car for the event to finish Jan saw some of the young helpers around a tall young man who she noticed had an occultish book on his lap.

She felt compelled to go over and talk with them.

As she explained that Jesus is greater than Satan, the young man started to remove an amulet from his neck. 'This gives me protection and power.' he said as he tried to put it round Jan.

Jan raised her hand and quietly said 'In the name of Jesus.', only to see him stagger backwards, and then retreat.

Not only did the young people then listen to what she had to say about Jesus, but ten of them gave their lives over to him.

- o O o -

What do you think of when someone mentions the word 'witch'? A wart-nosed hag - like in Macbeth? Grottbag on childrens' television? A black-capped Halloween figure on a broomstick?

Rosanne (not her real name) came to us as the result of someone sharing their faith with her at work. She was a sweet, vivacious, gentle, young mum trying hard to bring up her kids, just like any normal mum, but in fact she had been deeply involved in witchcraft, and was called a 'white witch'.

Thinking that white witches did good by good powers she had one day surprisingly found out that the source of her powers was the same 'guide' as a 'black witch' was using.

Gradually over the years the power base in her life had shifted, until what she thought she was in control of was controlling her. Held prisoner by evil, all she basically wanted, and needed, now was freedom - the freedom of Jesus.

Her work friend knew a bit about her past, and felt she would be out of her depth should 'something turn up.' so asked for some help. I was only one or two steps ahead of her myself!

We made an appointment with Rosanne, and hours before she arrived prayed hard together (asking two or three others we could trust beside our partners to also pray for us).

What do you think of when someone mentions the word 'witch'?

I think Satan wanted to put us in fear before we started, thinking that a combination of Ghostbusters/Omen 1, 2 & 3/ and Armageddon would result if we did anything against him with one of his servants.

First of all we explained to Rosanne that we are all, in different ways, influenced and controlled by Satan, no-one is any worse than any other, and that Jesus died to forgive us and free us whatever we are like or may have done.

After sharing the fact that because Jesus beat death (Satan's last post) he can deal with anything and anyone, we then asked her if she wanted to move out from under Satan's control into the love of Jesus. She said 'Yes.'

Rosanne found that first part fairly easy. After all she wanted to know Jesus. Having paused on the threshold of this momentous step she said sorry for her failures and wrongs, thanked Jesus for loving her enough to die for her and asked him into her life to be her Saviour.

It was the next bit that was hard.

'I want you to tell Satan that you don't want to be under his control any more, and tell Jesus that you renounce the Devil and all his works. You want Jesus to be Lord.'

You could see the inner struggle going on. There were no shrieks or screams, nothing violent - though you could see her fist clenching as though to strike out - no histrionics - just a rigidity in her body as she bent and backed away.

It was painful to watch. She just couldn't say it.

Eventually we decided to tackle that another day. The main thing was she had made Jesus her Saviour.

The battle was won, though the war was not yet over.

I now understand the reason for debriefing prisoners of war.

Over the following weeks that Rosanne's friend and I talked and prayed together with Rosanne we learned so much about Satan's crafty and destructive schemes.

We found out that Satanists have no problem in talking about 'the Lord', but when they say it they actually mean Satan. That's why Satan didn't want her to say that Jesus was Lord.

As Rosanne admitted her involvement with fortune telling, tarot cards, palmistry, etc., and renounced the occult powers behind them, areas of her life came out into the light of Jesus.

Over the next few week Rosanne was able to tell Jesus that HE was now her Lord.

Also we came to discover that behind the superficial were the deeper things, and behind the deeper things were the hidden, and behind the hidden were the real powers.

Satan was happy to let a spirit of divination go, even a spirit of witchcraft, as a cover for those demonic archangels of the earth, with specific names used in witchcraft ceremonies, to remain.

On our part, it wasn't by our efforts or forcefulness that

these went, but simply as we relied, called on, and used the name of our Lord Jesus.

The last to go was - I was going to say 'a real devil of a nuisance' - determined that he wasn't going to budge. But he had to, because, as we reminded him 'Rosanne now belongs to Jesus, he is now her Lord. You're a squatter.' Eventually he packed his bags.

A great deal of healing was needed in many inner and damaged areas of her life. But what a thrill to see the new Rosanne emerging out of the shadows.

I don't want to over-dramatise or under-state the facts, but when you are involved in building an outpost for the Kingdom of God someone has to lose territory. The loser is Satan, and he doesn't like it.

So one way or another there will be battles and those battles will mean problems.

But it's worth it.

Chapter 4

Basic Structures

I remember the first time I braved entering the builders' merchants on my own. I felt like a fish out of water as I eyed all those 'proper' builders.

I took a deep breath, looked at my list of materials to buy, and began bravely, 'Six metres of Denso tape, please.'

'What width?' intoned the man behind the desk without so much as lifting his head from the order sheet.

'I...I...I don't know. In fact I don't know what it is. You see', I confided, 'I'm a clergyman.'

He slowly raised his head, then raised an eyebrow in disbelief.

Crestfallen I returned home to find out more from our neighbour, David, who was advising me about the practicalities of building.

Starting a church family from nothing is a bit like that. You have to know what you want and what you mean.

There are problems in being on your own - even if you do have a wife, two teenage daughters, and a dog. You feel a bit isolated and lonely, very responsible, and a bit daunted, because the task is so enormous.

However, being on your own does have the advantage of not having to fulfil anyone's expectations, and you can start by asking basic questions - besides: 'What on earth am I doing here?'

The first question needs to be 'What is God's agenda?'

Soon behind that, especially when people start to get interested, comes the question 'What is a Church?'

When we left Devon people were saying things to us like 'When you have a Sunday School'...'Of course you will have a Sisterhood', and to Heather, who was a Girls Brigade Officer, 'We look forward to hearing about the 1st Bramingham Company.'

When we arrived in Luton people offered us things like a huge well-worn King James 'Pulpit Bible' and asked if we wanted a pedal organ.

I even inherited some provisional Site Plans of a church building with a 'Sanctuary' and two rooms to the side called 'Minister's Vestry' and 'Deacons' Vestry'.

Later we were given different sorts of Constitutions so that we could form, as someone pompously said, 'a proper church', even though that was three years after we had started meeting, and a year after we had approved our own simple constitution.

Is that what a church is - Organisations, Equipment, Buildings, and Rules and Regulations?

We had some hard praying and thinking to do in those early days.

As we squeezed into our front room (trying to avoid knocking over the guitars, tripping over the Overhead Projector lead, stepping on arthritic toes or children's fingers, and sending the songbooks flying all over the place) after singing a few lively songs that just about poleaxed all the aforementioned, the first bit of the Bible we looked at was Matthew 16:18 as we tried to answer the question 'What is a Church?'

Part of that question had been answered with, believe it or not, the man from the Rates Office the week before.

We had been in our home for a few months when the man from the Rates Office came to our house to visit and to assess it.

He had done a few calculations and gave his opinion with an officious air.

Fortunately Frank, the Beds. Baptist Association treasurer was there. 'But we are entitled to a special rate for this house. This is a church house.' he stated.

'Oh yes,' replied the man sensing a confidence trick 'then where is the church?'

That's a question that many people ask in another way. What is a church? When is a church a church?

'The church is here, and one day it will be there.' I said as I indicated, through the French windows and across the estate to Sainsbury's, the place where we would eventually meet.

He wasn't convinced.

'Look, my wife and family have come up from Devon, called by God to start a church here on this estate. Already we meet every Sunday for service here in this room, and have prayer meetings each week.'

'The council have allocated us a site to build a place of worship between the pub, Sainsbury's and the planned doctors surgery in the community area of this estate.'

He was wavering, so I pulled out my ace.

'I am a fully accredited clergyman, and have been so for the past seventeen years.'

That did it. The house was given church house status.

The following Sunday I said: 'Never forget: Church is about people. About you and me. We're all like Peter - stones or bricks - in the church that Jesus wants to build. We're all different, old and young (as I looked at Dorothy our OAP and Corrine who was just 5 years old), little and large (as I got Heidi, who was also 5 years old, and Val, a teacher who was an over 6'2" West Indian, to stand together) and Jesus loves us ALL, and wants to use us all.'

I put up on the OHP screen drawings of some typical notice boards seen outside churches.

'St. Mary's Church', 'Bunyan Meeting House', 'Weslyan Chapel'.

'Is it Mary's church, Bunyan's, Wesley's, or ours? ' I asked.
'No, Jesus says it's MY church.'

'We build on him. He builds with us.'

Right at the beginning we were establishing two basic Values[2] that have stayed with us right through to today.

First, the Lordship of Jesus - in our lives and in his church.

Second, the value of people - whoever, and whatever they are like.

It was out of these two values that, some time later, we created our Commitment Card which stated:

'Our Commitment is to Love - the Lord and obey his word

- one another as we are unconditionally

- those needing Jesus to bring them to know him.'[3]

After a time of open prayer and a few more songs we held

(2. See Appendix 1)
(3. See Appendix 2)

hands and sang the prayer churches call 'The Grace', then we said 'Thank You' for our food, and in came the sandwiches, cakes and jelly that we still enjoy today (not the same ones!)

One week, some new people came to our 3.30pm service. As we were tucking in to the food that people quite happily brought each week, they asked 'Who's the party for?' 'This is just our regular tea.' I explained 'We have this every week.'

'It's not like a church here' they said. 'It's more like a family.'

My heart leaped and shouted 'Bingo. We're on target.' Because that was what the Lord quite clearly told us to be at one of our earliest get-togethers. His actual words were 'Be my Family.'

With that phrase in mind we believed it was right that we should meet in the afternoon each Sunday for the sort of celebratory type of worship that all ages could join in (with questions and comments of all kinds - some weeks were hilarious!) and then have tea together as a family.

On the one hand we had no option because the A-frame that we moved into only had one 'L-shaped' room (besides a midgey kitchen and toilet) so we stayed together, OAPs, middleys, children, even babies as they were breast-fed in the middle of the service. But we stayed together more because we believed that the Lord wanted it that way.

Looking at the ministry of Jesus it seems as though he operated on two levels. Whenever he spoke to the crowds, which usually included the children, he was the Master Storyteller, but if anyone wanted to go further he would chat to them in small groups. Following this pattern, Sunday afternoons majored on Family Worship, and during the week small groups met to discuss and pray things through.

Everyone had to be very tolerant and adaptable, and learn to enjoy it if they, and we as a group, were going to survive.

At the end of another action packed afternoon, as young hands squashed her poor twisted arthritic fingers with the word 'Squeeze' that somehow had got added after singing the final 'Amen' of 'The Grace', Dorothy was heard to say one week, with her wise wry smile, 'This church is certainly stretching me.'

But that's how we grow.

Of course it's more comfortable not to be 'stretched', but unstretched muscles soon become so weak and powerless that they seize up.

That wasn't the only way that the Lord wanted to stretch us. He wanted to stretch us in service.

In so many churches, too often the cry goes up, 'We need a Sunday School teacher/Brigade Officer/Editor.' and the next new person in through the church doors gets grabbed and squeezed into the mould whether they fit or not. 'The need constitutes the call' is the theory behind that one! That's what often happens in 'normal' churches.

Well, we didn't intend to be 'normal' even though in the early days some people said that we 'needed' this and that 'Officer.' and one or two even suggested that they or their partner would be just right for the position.

We wanted to be obedient.

If we took one wrong step NOW we could end up miles away from where the Lord wanted us to be, because once a thing is done it sets a precedent that is difficult to change.

My constant reply was 'There's no need to rush.'

Going back to basics made me realise that the first thing people needed to do was to find out what gifts God had given or wanted to give to each individual.

As I studied my Bible afresh I came to see that 'service' grows from 'gifting', and 'leadership' out of 'service'.

So I prepared to talk about the gifts Jesus gives by his Spirit, and tried to get a team from a church more experienced in these things to take a day of workshops on this subject.

Have you ever thrown a sweet paper out of the front window of the car (by way of illustration of course!) only to find it come back in through the rear window. The advice I threw out now landed on my own back seat as I had to learn what I was telling others - no need to rush.

- o O o -

'What are we thinking about on these Sunday afternoons?'

At first there was no response. It's amazing how people pick up these caricatures of church life. The hush of holiness, the silence of a service.

'You are allowed to talk.' I said to the children, 3 teenagers, and 15 adults squashed into our front room. Out of the hubbub that followed arose the word 'church'.

Using the old illustration, I showed a sign with the letters 'CH—CH' on it.

'What's missing?'

'U.R.' chirped the children, then suddenly giggled as they thought about what they'd just said.

'What's missing'

'The church is incomplete when 'U.R.' missing - that means me or you.' I continued. 'Remember the other week when we said that Jesus loves us all, whether we are young or old, big or small, and wants us to be bricks in his church. What would you think about a house with some bricks missing?'

Various comments ensued about some of the buildings on the estate - 'Sounds like a ****** (name with held for legal reasons) home!' said someone to the laughter of everyone.

'Now who can read this?' I asked as I held up a large sheet of paper saying something like:

> 'Whxn wx arx not hxrx Jxsux sxxs,
> as wxll as mx and othxrs. It makxs
> thx lifx and sxrvicx of thx family
> xxtrxmly hard.'

'Not only are there gaps when we are not around, but then others try to fill in and make up what's missing and that makes life very difficult, because God made you different from me - aren't you glad?' Again various rude comments followed with gales of laughter rippling round the room.

'When we give our lives to Jesus he trusts us with 'gifts' of his Spirit so that we do his work and together make sense of what he is trying to say.'

So it was in those early days that the importance of 'gifting' was laid as a foundation block. This freed us up to use those gifts, whenever it was appropriate, in a very natural and easy way.

We'd already had a prophecy or two ('Be MY Family' for example), were starting to pray for the sick, and as mentioned earlier had needed to free people from Satan's grip.

But that which was 'apostolic' in one person (I had come to understand with my new eyes that an 'apostolic ministry' meant not heavy shepherding but God investing all the necessary gifts to a church planter to start a church) had to be released to the church family so that IT became apostolic. [4]

- o O o -

'Hello, how many have you brought with you this time?' asked Mary Pyches, the bishop's wife at St. Andrews, Chorleywood, in Middlesex.

I had made great friends with the folk at St. Andrews during my three month Sabbatical in 1982. I called it my 'second spiritual home' for a number of reasons, not least because of the way they'd welcomed me with genuine friendship, linked me in with one of their home groups, let me be me - not a clergyman on retreat but an ordinary person - and helped me to understand and experience what I call 'the supernatural in a natural way'. They then nurtured me gently through a spiritual 'time-warp' after an unexpected 'power encounter' with the Holy Spirit. (Wow, that was a mouthful - but so was my time with them, it was gob-stopping!)

Heather had come to love Mary for the gentle, wise and

---

[4] See Appendix 9

powerful ministry of 'inner healing' from many past hurts and hindrances in her life that Mary had exercised over a number of weeks of counselling.

St. Andrews really was our second home.

That's why we took as many of our church family as we could down the M1 and round the M25 for their monthly 'Teach-ins' on 'How to minister in the power of the Holy Spirit' so that they could experience it for themselves.

We didn't want to copy St. Andrews, but see what God was doing, and hear what he had to say to us. Some things we took on board, others we didn't. But what a privilege to learn in such an atmosphere.

I loved to sit at the front - where the action was - and taught others to do the same.

Some time later we had a team come to us from Chorleywood to take a day of teaching and celebration so that we could all be let loose to serve the Lord Jesus in his way.

Encounter with Christ, gifting, service, leadership - that's the pattern.

So then leadership came later, much later, as Heather will tell you:

- o O o -

'Early on, while we were still in the A-frame, we began to think and pray about the whole concept of leadership. Obviously as the church grew bigger there would need to be leaders - but who, and how?

The earliest attempt at finding God's leaders for the emerging church family was later scrapped, but the findings were interesting.

I spoke personally to 30 people, 22 of whom had signed the 1987 'covenant' that signified that they were committing themselves to be God's family on Bramingham Park (most of the others subsequently did). I asked each person who they felt were best equipped to be leaders of the church. More specifically, who did they feel were in touch with God and in touch with people. They were asked to write down the names of 2 or 3 people, or even 7 or 8 if they felt it appropriate, who were walking with the Lord and concerned for spiritual things, and to whom people could easily relate.

When all 30 had done this we 'sat' on the list of names because we weren't sure that this was the right way of going about things. But it is interesting to see how 7 out of the first 9 names given did eventually become leaders IN the church, not OF the church, as they later became leaders of teams.

It occurred to us that just to choose leaders, however good, and then to find jobs for them to do seemed to be the wrong way round. We both had the conviction that leadership had to arise out of 'gifting' and 'service'. It had to be from the grass roots up not an imposed hierarchy coming down.

There was certainly plenty of work to be done. Up to this point we had muddled along, many helping in different ways as they were able.

Meg played on her flute on Sundays, encouraging Rachel to play hers sometimes. Ryder and I strummed guitars.

Both in our home and in the A-frame people took turns at washing up. Andrew Fox, one of the dads, became an expert at getting well drenched in the process.

People were beginning to pray for and with one another.

Ryder kept a record of the offerings and gifts in a little red book, and plastic bags of money were labelled and kept with great care in a corner of the bedroom. Once a month he would total up the cost of hiring the A-frame for so many hours, and pop across the road to Eric (the rent collector for the A-frame) with a bag of small change. Excess money would then be taken to Frank, and later to the bank, and be put into an account set up by the Beds. Association for the church.

People were starting to care for each other pastorally and to share their faith with those who had not yet found Christ.

Although somewhat haphazardly and apparently disorganized to tidier minds, things were getting done as we felt our way forward.

Newcomers wanted to know how they could fit in and serve the Lord. 'Pray and wait for him to show you.' was the inevitable advice.

One weekday morning I sat down with a sheet of paper

and listed all the tasks that needed to be done, and the opportunities of service that there were. I grouped the jobs under main headings, and found that there were 11 main groups.

A friend called and suggested that we added 'Youth Team', which I eagerly did without too much thought (not realising at the time that 'Youth' denoted age rather than service, and that by the same token we might as well have had an 'Elderly' team or 'Women's team'). Eventually this petered out, as did a 'Representatives' team (for Women's World Day of Prayer, Missionary Representatives etc.).

People were all given a sheet entitled 'Work and Faith sharing in the Church Family.'[5] They were encouraged to pray about this and tick a box or two indicating what they felt might be their gifting, God's leading, or their area of interest, and to return the form complete with their name to Ryder or me.

After a few weeks, when most of the forms were back (though some were being prayed over some months later) I made lists of people under each team heading and gave each individual the appropriate list or lists with their name on.

For example 10 people had ticked the Pastoral box because they wanted to care for others in such ways as sick visiting, letter writing, welcoming new people at church, taking flowers to new mums or the bereaved etc. Each of these 10 was given a piece of paper with all 10 names on it and asked to organise a meeting of the group, then when it was fixed to ask Ryder to come to it. This way we were not pre-selecting leaders, but those with leadership gifts tended to arrange the meetings and get things going. Once the meeting occurred members could see each other and know a sense of 'we are in this together'! First they started to get to know each other, pray together, and then discuss what the areas of need might be.

So team profiles began.[6]

After meeting two or three times team members were asked to pray about who might be God's choice from among the people in that particular team to lead them spiritually and practically for the year ahead. In other words, who had a gift of leadership as well as a pastoral gift?

---

(5) See Appendix 3
(6) See Appendix 4

Eventually another meeting was called when each person wrote privately on their own piece of paper who they felt was God's choice. Only Ryder saw those papers. The vast majority chose Anne, who quite honestly would never have chosen the job for herself or considered herself suitable.

This all took time.

Gradually, over several months, leaders for each team were 'chosen'. In each case the person's name was brought to 'talkback' (the church's praying and sharing forum) when the church family was asked to pray during the next month, until the next 'talkback', to see if they could confirm that this was God's man/woman for the job.

When the church had 'owned' this person, at the next family communion the leader was prayed over and set aside for their work. Two or three people would join Ryder in praying for the Lord's anointing and enabling.

As the leaders were 'chosen', almost by accident a Leadership Team was created. This group began to meet for prayer, support, and encouragement on a monthly basis. These times were not business meetings but primarily times of prayer support, enabling every area of church life to be prayed over, and for any particular struggles a leader might be having to be shared with others who were also learning.

Mutual understanding and help was given.

Despite some drawbacks we found enormous advantages in this kind of leadership (See Appendix 5 for further discussion). While this may not be God's plan for other churches in other areas, we are sure that this is how he wants it here and now at Bramingham.'

- o O o -

'Parsley. I need some parsley. I've got the lettuce, horse-radish sauce, baked egg, salt water, wine, lamb's bone, motzas, charoseth, candles, and Bible, but I NEED some parsley.' I groaned.

We were going to have a Passover Party.

It was great on Maundy Thursday to go through the sort of events that Jesus and his disciples shared in. The songs, the scriptures, and the symbols. To be a sort of Jewish Family.

We not only celebrated the Passover but with it - Communion.

But before we shared in the meal, just as Jesus did, I took a towel and filled a bowl with water.

'Who's going to have their feet washed?'

People giggled, more out of embarrassment then anything else.

One lady volunteered.............. her husband.

'You can.' she laughingly stated, pointing to her husband. 'You washed your feet before you came out.' Maybe she made this suggestion for my sake thinking of other smelly feet.

'The water's warm.' I said encouragingly as I took his large West Indian foot in my white hands and washed first the one foot then the other.

'Jesus came not to be served but to serve.' I quoted. and secretly thought 'Yes. This is what leadership is about. Not power but service.'

Chapter 5

Bricks and Bits

We had been negotiating for possession of the site for our church building for what seemed ages.

Yes, it was ours, the developers kept re-iterating. Yes, we would get it.

Yes, the price was still the same (a miracle, as land prices were increasing daily). Yes, they would release the land soon.

But when?

'Into your hands He'll give the ground you claim.' came the words of the song written by Graham Kendrick[7] as one day we were praying about this problem.

'Let's go for it.' I encouraged the church family.

'How?' asked someone.

'You pray and I'll ask the developers if we can start by putting a cross on the site where the church building will be....some day!.... and then I'll ask them if we can have a Good Friday service there.'

After one or two 'phone calls they eventually agreed. Prayer, we learned in a practical way, was able to move the obstacles that had held the land back for so long.

Pioneer Church Planters have to be so versatile - faith sharers, door to door visitors, Bible teachers, musicians ....gardeners!

People at the start of Holy Week saw me stripped off, not to carry a cross but with my Flymo Hover mower held waist high above my shorts and wellie boots to scythe through the rough grass and weeds that covered the plot where the church would one day stand.

We'd already got the plans in hand for the church, so I cut more carefully and closely in the undergrowth the basic shape of the property in the appropriate place - and imagined what it would be like when the building would be there in all its glory.

Then on Good Friday a couple of dozen of us met outside the Sales Information Office where we usually held our Sunday

---

(7) Rejoice! © 1983 Thankyou Music

services.

Slowly we marched behind an eight foot cross with banners flying proclaiming the Easter message 'Christ has died', 'Christ is risen', 'Christ will come again'.

We marched across the main road, past the pub (much to the amusement of people drinking in the garden) around Sainsbury's and onto our site to hold an open air service there.

After meditating on Christ's cross as 'a spectacle for the world', we sank our wooden cross into the ground and nailed it down - not realising that it would stand there unvandalised for nearly a year.

The husband of one of our ladies who regularly frequented the pub (the husband I mean) forcefully stated, 'Let anyone touch that cross and they'll have me to answer to.'

Thankfully, no one did.

- o O o -

As far as building was concerned I was a total novice.

I didn't know the difference between a soffit and a screed, 6 foot of PSE from a 2 metre RSJ, a Yorkshire 'T' fitting from a sliding truss clip, or a fletton from a piece of flashing.

'Build a Church!' my mother giggled (she was probably remembering the dog kennel I had made in Devon that weighed a ton, was large enough for the dog and our daughters to get in and was held together with about a hundred screws) '...you couldn't build a shed!'

But God knew otherwise. He was the Boss and he had it all in hand.

Already he had given us John, who was a construction engineer, and David, our neighbour who was both an architect in the Council offices and who had built his own house.

'What's the church going be like?' was the question many people frequently asked us as the time got nearer to build.

'What do you think it should be like?' was the reply we threw back.

Gradually a whole number of suggestions were collected from our imaginative church family that, from the youngest to the oldest, blossomed with ideas.

Together the three of us (David, John and I) studied the ideas given to us by the people who were regular attenders. After putting to one side some of the more impractical suggestions, we drew up a rough plan.

These ideas were then sent to Alistair.

Alistair was an Architect. He was a member of a new church that he had designed himself in Thatcham. We thought that if he was happy to sit in his own church, he could draw up all the specifications for ours.

Meanwhile we made application to the Luton Planning Office for our church.

And waited.

'It's there. It's there in the local paper,' someone 'phoned to say, early one morning, 'It's in there with all the other applications.'

I hurriedly dropped the phone and grabbed the local freebie. It read 'L/10435/R/9 Erection of a church, Whitehorse Vale, Bramingham Park.'

How exciting to receive a long blue cardboard tube with all the detailed plans and specifications from our architect, and later get full planning permission from the Council and the green light to go ahead.

Being the innocent that I was I thought that we'd have everything built in the next twelve months, and booked Lou Lewis, a Christian song-writer and singer, for the following year to take a gospel concert in our new building.

It was going to take a lot longer than that - in fact nearly two years just to get in.

- o O o -

As a matter of policy we decided to build the church ourselves.

First of all so as to provide an opportunity to show and share our faith. Men who would not come to a service, probably might come on site.

Second, because we didn't have enough money, and God hadn't promised us half a millions pounds (unfortunately!). All we had at the time was £30,000 given by people in the Beds.

Baptist Association, our own folk, friends, and a number of other churches - £20,000 for the land, and £10,000 to build, but that was enough to get us started.

Despite the apprehension expressed by departments of the Baptist Union that we shouldn't think of starting with such a small sum we said that God would provide.

To their credit, as soon as we had drawn up the plans for the property and put in our application for building permission to the local authority the BU released a further £50,000 in grants - a £25,000 loan to be repaid after 5 years and another £25,000 non-returnable loan (though I could never understand how a loan could be non-returnable). The rest came in through the sacrificial giving of our own little but growing family and those people who took us to their hearts.

In the end we built the whole complex for less than £98,000 - after all the hard work of claiming back the VAT!

o - O - o

25th May 1988 will be forever engraved on my heart.

I can still visualize John with his theodolite, David with his tape measure, and me with a hammer and some wooden stakes, striding through the rough grass to measure levels and lengths and bash in those pieces of wood.

Then, there was Mick from round the corner. David knew him as a friend who had helped him years earlier when David had built his own house. The day following our marking out - a Saturday - Mick arrived on site and really made an impression with his bulldozer.

As he started site-stripping people stopped and stared.

'What's going on?' was the question of the curious.

'We are building our church.' we excitedly replied.

By 'we' I meant every willing person, no matter what their age, sex, or ability. The principle of 'Be My Family' extended to Saturdays as well.

Looking back, although we were exceptionally safety conscious, I dread to think what any building inspector might have said if he had turned up some Saturdays and seen us balancing like ballerinas from various bits of the property. But more about that later.

For me the excitement grew as Mick cut into the subsoil and exposed that white chalk which had been the prophecy and confirmation of our call to Luton. There is nothing like being where the Lord wants you to be.

After the site had been levelled David, John and I returned to peg out the foundation footings that would mark the actual shape of the future building.

One evening that week as I looked out from my study window I noticed someone wandering about on site, so I quickly popped over to see what was going on.

It turned out to be a little man with a metal detector.

I smiled and asked 'Excuse me, what are you doing?'

This amateur archeologist explained his interest and showed me a buckle and a Roman coin. I didn't have the heart to say that he was trespassing and that the find should be handed over to us.

But I did recognise the coin. It was a Roman 'lepta' called in the Bible 'the widow's mite'. It seemed significant that such a small coin as Jesus noticed for the way it was sacrificially given not how big it was should be unearthed on our site.

It reminded me that the Lord is pleased with us no matter how small a group we are and happy whatever we give no matter how small it is, as long as it's with all our heart.

We were being asked to give in a similarly sacrificial way in time, energy and money, and would surely know Jesus' smile of approval.

- o O o -

Ray lived less than a hundred yards away from our home, in fact just up the top of our road.

In his front garden was a JCB.

Ray had done contract work for different building developers on our estate virtually since day one of the estate.

He had also built his own beautiful house on Bramingham Park. His JCB was usually standing idle on Saturdays on his drive, and so as a neighbour he said that he was willing to work for us 'at cost'. A trench that would have cost £300 he did for £50.

To get things going he turned up late on the following Friday evening after Mick's site strip and started to cut out a few metres of chalk. He then parked his machine on site so as to start early next morning.

It looked really impressive - mounds of earth and chalk, and our own JCB.

Most weekends as we worked away, people stopped and watched. Again we were able to talk about the future, and about our faith. Sometimes Ray and I sat and talked alone over a mug of tea about Ireland, religion, and how only Jesus brings real peace and harmony to people's hearts and the nations.

Ray, this quiet Irishman, was so helpful and unassuming.

He not only cut out the footings with his JCB, but got down into them with his spade and helped us and the children clean them out. Every loose bit of chalk had to be removed so that the foundations would be strong and pass inspection.

- oOo -

Normally a building inspector would not come out on a Saturday. But the chief Building Officer, being a friend of our David, came out specially to check and pass our trenches, as well as to give us a few helpful bits of advice.

As the site had a slight gradient we had to make 'shuttering' (a bit like steps) to stop the cement that was to be poured in from pouring out.

To save money, we collected scrap wood from the different builders' rubbish piles to make this shuttering for our foundations. The various site foremen grinned as the 'vicar' pestered them for this and that again.

I telephoned many firms to get the best price for ready-mix concrete for the foundations. I was beginning to become quite a dab hand at all this negotiating and getting a bargain.

Like the time (much later) when we needed to purchase all our electric cable, sockets, plugs and lights. I went to one electrical merchants and asked for a quote. I went to another firm (telling them about the first) which they bettered. I then went to a third who bettered the second, and finally returned to the first who now dropped their original price lower than the last so saving us 30% from their earlier quote.

The following Saturday after doing all the shuttering, with a bunch of men, women and children - and feeling like a kid on holiday with a huge present waiting to be unwrapped on Christmas Day - I waited for the lorries to come and 'shoot' the dark grey river of cement into the white channels we had prepared.

The lorries arrived every 45 minutes - five of them. Well, in fact, six because one had to be sent back - they had forgotten to put cement in with the aggregate!

Bob, our own builder, spotted it just in time as it started pouring out of the huge rotating drum.

'Hold it mate,' he yelled at the driver 'you've forgotten something.'

The delay gave us time to 'puddle' the cement (this is done by pumping poles up and down to remove air pockets in the cement - as opposed to 'paddling' with feet, which was strictly forbidden). Then we carefully placed below the surface the reinforcing mesh where the steel columns were to stand.

The children loved plopping their sticks and poles into the grey mixture to get the air out.

Whoops of delight filled the air as one of the Dads disobeyed the instructions we had given to the children. He tried to jump over the setting cement and landed wellie deep in one trench. Even more of a delight as he was one of the local school teachers.

At the end of the day, glowing with exertion and excitement, we wandered round the black 'T' shape that stood out so clearly in the white chalk. You could really begin to dream dreams about what the place would be like.

It seemed so huge after our cramped condition in the A-frame which would fit three times into just the main hall we were building.

- o O o -

Something I learned early was forward planning. Things had to be ready on site for the next stage, like for example the

He ... landed wellie-deep in one trench

bricks and cement. But the question was where could we store them - not by our house!

Once again God answered our prayers and came up trumps.

One Saturday evening David said that one of the building firms on the estate had discarded a couple sheds that were gradually getting buried under grass on a corner of the estate. The better of the two was made of wood while the other was an old corrugated metal one.

Off I trotted and found the foreman.

'Do you need both those old sheds?' I asked hopefully, thumbing a blistered digit at a pile of what looked like rubbish.

'Why?' he asked after vetting this dishevelled character with an inquisitive and suspicious look.

'For the church we are building' I announced proudly.

'Oh that' he replied with an amused grin - our reputation was spreading amongst the professionals.

'We need something to store our goods in and if ....'

'OK,' he said without pausing, 'you can have the metal one. Though it's not all there.' he added as an afterthought, remembering that he was talking to a 'man of God'.

Three quarters of an hour later we were back with a dumper truck that Ray had borrowed for us from one of the sites where he was working that month.

As we balanced huge panels of metalwork on the tipper part and bumped across the ground and briefly onto the road, spreading well over the middle markings, I prayed that we wouldn't meet any vehicles or drop anything on the way.

Backwards and forwards we went 'til we had everything on our site.

As I drove the dumper through the advancing twilight back to its owners it was then that I suddenly wondered if my driving licence allowed me to drive this thing on the road. Quickly I bumped up onto the pavement and across the fields.

The next Saturday we had great fun puzzling out what parts fitted where. Eventually we managed to erect a site shed like none other. It ended up half its original size and needed a few new panels of corrugated metal that I purchased from the builders merchants and brought back balanced on a blanket on the roof of my estate car.

That shed lasted us over three years, and had only two break-ins.

The first time we lost all our tools. That was sad as they were personally owned by our helpers and therefore had many special memories and sentimental value.

Thankfully we were covered by insurance so were able to claim on our policy. The money wasn't really enough to replace everything, but a salesman at one of the building merchants who we had got to know quite well and was always asking how the church was going, gave us a very good deal, enabling us to replace most things

- o O o -

David next introduced me to another of his friends who ran a brick library.

There we pondered the colours, strengths, shapes and prices for different types and makes of bricks that were standing together on special shelves like a real library.

On one of my many visits there the senior manager, having heard that we were building a church, took me into his office for a cuppa, and before long we were talking about spiritual things.

With this new knowledge about bricks we bought some strong but bargain 'rejects' for the foundations, and from another merchant the main wall bricks which were to cover inside as well as outside, and then some red smooth 'facing' specials to decorate round the windows and doors and cover the columns we had to build on the inside.

Just after we had ordered the bulk of our wall bricks the price unexpectedly shot up and availability suddenly became delayed by six months due to one of the construction firms on our estate deciding to use the same bricks as we had chosen.

God's timing is perfect.

How the other building foremen envied our immediate deliveries while they had to wait.

Another bonus for us was when we ran out of bricks and needed some unobtrusive ones I was able to go over to the foreman of the houses that were being built with our 'Peppercorn' bricks and beg any that he didn't want. He let me dig through their huge mound of rejects and pile them into the back of my estate car - for free. Backwards and forwards I went and by this method was able to save us from buying over two hundred more bricks.

- o O o -

Another of God's gifts to us was Gary.

Gary was a Christian and a member of a nearby Baptist church. He turned up one Saturday to say that he'd heard about us and wondered if he and his firm of two other men could help.

David and I had worked out that, if we did the brickwork ourselves, at the pace we were going by working only on Saturdays, it would take us at least an extra nine months. So here was another answer to prayer.

On a Christian gentleman's agreement (just a shake of hands and a prayer) Gary agreed a fair price to do the foundations and walls, as he said, 'I want to do it for the Lord.'

His two workers weren't Christians, so it was great to sit down with them after lugging round bricks and cement bags together, to have a coffee break and a chat about the Lord. Gary, the boss, didn't mind if we went on a bit. He was so glad to have a clear opportunity to share his own faith with his mates.

Gary, as a Christian, went the extra mile. He 'pointed' the brickwork for nothing because he thought it would 'look nicer', made a cross with contrasting colour bricks high up on the wall facing the school, and then at the end of the job gave his last week of work free as his 'tithe to the Lord'.

As the building went up the Lord did all sorts of other wonderful things for us to encourage our faith and witness.

- o O o -

It had been a wet week, though every Saturday for the two years it took us to do the external work it was fine. We didn't have to stop once.

Early that Saturday morning a lorry arrived with some more materials we had ordered and backed up to the church.

'It's muddy.' I warned.

'No sweat.' he said, though he said something else later when he attempted to get off site.

'What is this place?' he asked, as he tried to decipher the delivery note that said Bramingham Park Church. 'It's our church building,' I explained for the umpteenth time.

After unloading he tried to drive off site but the more he accelerated the deeper the lorry sank down into the mud, and the more exasperated he got.

'It'll take a bloody miracle to get this thing out now.' he exploded.

'OK God, if that's what we need then this is your chance and your place.' I quietly prayed. In less than a minute the 'phut phut' of a dumper truck was heard coming round the corner as one of the workman from another part of the estate arrived at the newspaper shop opposite us to purchase a bottle of cold Coke and his Saturday's copy of the Sun.

After a polite request he came over, put a chain onto the lorry, and in less than a minute had pulled the lorry out the mud.

'That was fortunate.' our lorry driver commented.

'No it wasn't.' I replied as I pointed heavenwards 'I asked The Boss'. The lorry driver left shaking his head, but he was smiling.

That wasn't the only occasion the Lord did that sort of thing.

Our roof trusses were delivered early one morning from Salisbury.

Some were A-shaped and pre-made to fit our 'upstairs' into. They were nine metres long and used wood thirty centimetres deep and seven and a half centimetres thick. I had not anticipated their weight. I thought we would off load them by hand. No way, not with just the three us us who turned up.

'Lord, we need a fork lift truck.' I desperately prayed, as the lorry driver looked from these amateurs to his watch and back again.

Within two minutes a fork lift arrived on the way to the pub opposite. After offering to pay for his drinks he off loaded all thirty in a matter of minutes. Hallelujah.

Things and people always seemed to arrive at the right time.

At the start there was our neighbour David Cham the architect. Then there was John Keble one of our members who was a construction engineer and surveyor; Mick and Ray with their digger and JCB. Bob Keble (John's Dad) a builder and decorator; Peter Hindmarche from Alistair's church in Thatcham who was a plasterboard fitter (he volunteered to do the difficult main hall ceiling with his wife just when we needed someone, and showed us in the process how to do the rest); John Deveney a roofer and tiler who helped us do the roof.

Then there was Alf, a local plumber who, because of a heart condition, had been told to stop work, but was depressed by inactivity.

The very day we said that we need someone to help with the plumbing for the church before laying the screed Alf turned up and simply said 'Do you need a plumber - for free?' he added.

He told us his situation and how the friendly doctor from the surgery opposite the church had suggested that he needed an interest, and maybe could advise us in our work. 'But' Alf warned us 'No talking religion, or I'm off.'

We kept to the bargain for six months until he began to ask

questions about the Christian faith. Eventually eighteen months later after a major heart operation he confessed that he had trusted the Lord for himself just before his op.

In the meantime he helped us to do the plumbing for the water, install the toilets (nine of them), the boiler and all the radiators, as well as tile the floor of the toilets and lots more.

Then there was Paul, later to become our son-in-law, a security alarm installer who put in the church alarm system and all the electrics. Earlier his alarm business had folded due to a recession, so he worked many extra days on the church on the roof, bolting together the roof trusses, felting and preparing for the tiles, whilst in his spare time looking for work for himself.

Early on, when they first met, he was taken by our youngest daughter, Rachel, to a Christian Rock Concert, where he gave his heart to the Lord Jesus. But part of it he also gave to our daughter.

Theirs was the first wedding in the church.

On the actual day of their wedding the electricity was still coming in on emergency supply. All the electrics for the whole church and service were working off of just one 13amp plug!!

Then there was the man who watched us from the newsagents opposite, after we had laid the silver sand base for the block paving entrance to the church and were considering apprehensively what to do next.

'This is how you do it.' he said as he wandered over to us. 'Laying block paving is my job.' After fifteen minutes professional instruction, and learning a few tips on the way, we were off - thanks to this unknown benefactor.

And what can we say about Fred, who came at his wife's bidding to do an afternoon's work and stayed for a year (not all the time!). And Pete who also at his wife's suggestion worked solidly for a year. Both wives were members of the church but found their husbands reluctant to come to church. Now they virtually lived there!!

And then there were all the church members, men and women and children, who slaved away Saturday by Saturday moving bricks and tiles, clearing and filling trenches, cutting and sorting wood, carrying and finding nails - a veritable army of willing volunteers.

Those who weren't able to do much physical work kept us plied with tea, coffee, hot dogs and pasties out of the back of a car.

By working together on our own place of worship first of all meant that we owned it as ours.

Secondly we learned the benefits of working together as a team (though the team was different every week) and how despite ignorance and weakness we were able to accomplish far more than doing things on our own.

And most important of all, we depended on the Lord. We had to!

While we were building the site was regularly filled with songs of praise.

Especially on occasions like the time John was working 'downstairs' cutting wood while others were balancing on the beams 'upstairs' - four metres up amongst the roof trusses - nailing supports together. Out of the blue John suddenly thought 'I really ought to put my safety hat back on'. Less than a minute later a claw hammer slipped out of someone's grip upstairs and landed right on the top of his hat, Crack. Thank God not his head.

A more formal time of praise was our third Easter when, after another March of Witness around the estate, we paraded with banners flying into the church which sounded like a tall ship in full sail due to the roofing felt flapping in the rising breeze. It felt like the sea as we ended up standing in puddles of water that had come though the open frame-less windows and doors.

There, we celebrated our crucified yet risen Saviour with songs and readings. The service culminated in screwing the battered old cross, that had stayed outside for over a year, onto the wall just over the place where it had stood to 'claim the ground' now given.

However with all the work done on the building other things suffered.

The evangelistic work suffered. The door to door visiting slackened off considerably. Though by working on the church building we had different opportunities for sharing our faith.

Pastoral work suffered as people spent so much time and energy on site and were very tired. However, friendships deepened as we worked side by side.

So, maybe after all things didn't suffer so much, they merely changed direction.

Unfortunately the health of many did suffer - what with bad backs, strained muscles, blooded hands and faces etc. After all, we weren't experts. But I suppose another flip side was that it gave the prayer ministry team a lot of practice.

Chapter 6

Building Up

One day we were down inside a deep a hole that Ray had dug with his JCB setting out the drains when a curious girl in her twenties leaned over and asked what we were doing.

For the 'nn'th time we explained that we were building a church building for our church family and for the estate.

'What will it be like?' she asked.

When we explained that, to identify with the estate and people on it, it would look something like a cross between the pub and the doctors she exclaimed in horror 'That's not a church. A church needs a spire, and to look like ..... a church.'

It's amazing how even the young can have such narrow preconceived ideas.

But there's the problem. Folks equate 'church' with property - often of a historic nature. Look at how non church goers get all offended if their parish church decides to alter its appearance in any way. Some parishioners even go to court about a place they rarely, if ever, attend. 'The vicar wants to spoil OUR church' they wail. Often church is thought of in terms of an ancient monument.

Remember the Rate man's question 'Where is your church?' and our reply, 'The church is people not property'?

When the Bible says 'Christ loved the church and gave himself for it.' it doesn't mean he died to give recognition to a load of bricks and mortar, he gave himself for the living stones that make US into his church.

Despite this, people do like to see a special - what they call - 'consecrated' place with mystical areas called 'chancels' and 'naves', 'sanctuaries' and 'vestibules'. Often they want to identify with Something visible rather than be identified with Someone invisible. And with the Something sadly many people get too attached to the place and the pew.

I remember in one of my churches a lady in her 90's who insisted on sitting in the same seat although there wasn't another person within spitting distance. 'I was brought to this pew as a baby, and I will die here.' she proudly announced, much to my fear that one Sunday she might.

At the start of our work in Luton when people on our expanding estate were invited to 'come to church' some initially found it hard to meet in a home, though those that did, came to love the informality and flexibility of it all.

Then, when we moved, they found it hard worshipping in a Sales Information Office.

The first Sunday when we met in the A-frame, some of our ladies tried to make it more churchy by wearing coats and hats throughout the service. Mischievously I turned the heat up on the Calor gas stove to maximum so that by the time we were half way through the service it was so hot they couldn't possibly bear to wear all these extras that they normally hadn't bothered about before anyway.

So the church which started in our front room, and moved to the A-frame, eventually settled into the property we had taken three years to build.

Maybe now, people thought, even though the property was not finished, at last they had come to a place where they could put their feet up (not literally I hasten to add) and get settled in. They were soon to be disappointed.

Often I had to remind us all that even when God's pilgrim people got into the promised land there was no rest. They had to possess the land. Rest doesn't come 'til heaven.

One of the things we tried to do was to avoid patterns that people get familiar with. Familiarity produces the 'comfort feel' and comfort leads to carelessness.

Design can play a large part in what we believe a church to be.

When we moved into our DIY church property, we built it to be multi-purpose. That meant that we had no church furnishings (platform, communion table, bishop's chair etc.). To add to this I tried to move the front of the service around as much as possible.

Just when people were getting used to the setting out of chairs and tables in a particular way we would turn everything round facing another wall, or arrange the chairs differently.

After two years of rotating changes one lady came to service and said 'Oh no! I thought we had tried everything, and now he's found yet another way'. This time the chairs had been put in a circle around a circular table for a communion in the round.

At least no-one could say 'That's my seat.' and leave their Bible there - they'd never know where it would be the next week.

Such change is unsettling, but is good as it stops us depending on the familiar.

In fact, as soon as we moved in to our church property, I began to explain that where we were now meeting for worship wasn't meant to be the end of our vision. So immediately we began to plan our 'upstairs'.

I talked about plans to fill our first place of worship then how we could start our third stage of development. For this we should think about building on to the base of our 'T' shaped property (looking down on it from above) to make it into an 'H' with an even larger meeting room for over 500 people.

Because that extension would be on a slope we envisaged a couple of shops underneath where we could have a Christian Bookshop and a Hairdressers for one of our members who had a mobile business and just loved to talk to her captive clients about her faith. Or maybe, someone suggested, a Coffee Shop called Crumbs.

What does the Bible say? Without a vision we perish. Even if we don't perish we certainly petrify.

Churches need to be constantly building, developing and growing.

We were doing that physically (with our property) and spiritually (with the people).

This was evident in the way our members invested their lives in one another.

Diane bubbled with life, always smiling and praising the Lord - though not like some of those grinny Christians who put it on. She was for real.

She was the travelling hairdresser who loved to have a captive audience in her hands.

She came to us, frustrated in a more traditional church where her two children struggled against going. They so loved coming to our church that now she could say 'If you don't behave you

WON'T go to church' A novel threat!

Where ever she went she would tell people how good the Lord was, she was a natural gossiper of the good news.

However she wasn't one of those pious super-spiritual types - so heavenly minded to be of no earthly use. When she saw a need she tried to do something about it.

Like the time when our washing machine broke down and she came round to our house, pinched all the washing (despite Heather's protests) and returned it the next day duly washed and ironed.

Many times our home was a bit like Victoria Station in the rush hour. If it wasn't a service or a Bible study, it was a children's club, or a counselling centre. And then there were the friends that our daughters brought home. One night we had fourteen of them camping with sleeping bags in the front room - boys divided from girls by a curtain, which didn't stop the occasional water pistol shot or cake from flying from side to side.

Every week the young mums studying Jonah and Malachi came with their babies and toddlers, gurgling and dribbling etc. on the carpet under my manly supervision (the babies I mean, not the mothers - gurgling I mean not 'under my supervision'. Sorry I'd better get back to where I was).

Once a month the Rainbow Club had a party in our front room. This generally ended up with sausages and baked beans or fish fingers and chips, followed by jelly and ice-cream smothered with 100's & 1000's or chocolate rice crispy cakes. When sometimes over 30 children had left the room it was like entering a war zone.

'Saint, Saint, tea time.' we would call out to motivate our mobile vacuum cleaner to sniff for and snaffle up all the crushed leftovers on the carpet and under the chairs.

Occasionally we had a ladies dinner - a three course sit down meal - with a guest speakers to talk about their life and faith. But more about that later.

Heather and I believed it right to practice an 'open house' policy for all and sundry - and both 'All' and 'Sundry' came quite frequently. Church planters can't afford to be too private. And we are grateful to our girls, Dawn and Rachel, for supporting us in this. It was a cost to them as well as us.

With all this going on it was a unexpected surprise then when Carol, a young mum with four children of her own, came round with her Shake & Vac and liberally distributed the stuff about, singing to the Lord while she vacuumed our downstairs. She told us that the Lord had spoken to her about 'washing the disciples feet' but felt that cleaning our floor would probably be more helpful.

We weren't the only beneficiaries of this growing sense of community. People in the church frequently went round to one another, loaning things, and helping out with practical jobs.

But at times building and developing real caring relationships can be costly in both price and pride.

....the Lord had spoken to her about 'washing the disciples feet' but felt that cleaning our floor would probably be more helpful

Asif came to Christ from a Muslim family. He and his wife, Pauline, with their two children Michael and Christopher moved onto our estate and soon fitted into the church family.

Asif had been working as a Sales Rep for a chemical firm. Life had been great - a company car and the potential to earn lots of money. Then sitting in his car one lunchtime God spoke to him about counting all things loss for Christ's sake to know him.

Feeling strongly that he should study accountancy to further his career he enrolled in the local College to do a course in Business studies.

Then a little while later the the Lord opened a door for him to begin 'at the bottom' at a Christian Housing Association in their finance department.

The 'bottom' not only meant no company car but a 50% cut in his wage packet. Was this what the Lord meant by 'counting all things loss'?

After a probationary two months he received a pay rise which brought him to a level where he could just about afford to pay the bills and feed the family - just about.

Asif's finances were well and truly stretched, and though a car would help the expense of travelling for the family, and him going to work in London by train (using more precious pounds) no way was that a possibility for him.

Over those initial two years individual people from the church dropped envelopes through his letterbox with gifts of money, or left bags with food in on their doorstep.

Through out this time the church family had been praying for Asif and his family. We all felt that this new job was right for him to take. But what about the car? A number of us believed that if the job was God's will for Asif then we should practically support him with an interest free loan so as he could buy the vehicle he needed.

When Asif questioned our unusual suggestion we simply said: 'Look. Our money isn't ours, it's the Lord's, and he has told us to to this, just like he is saying take the job. This is all part of being his family'

Asif gratefully accepted the loan, took the job, and within a short while was able to pay back the loan.

How easy it would have been for him to be proud and say no to our offer. How easy for the church to have been prayerful but not practical and left him car-less.

We were all learning that relationships are cemented when we do things, not when we talk about them.

Building relationships that are real can be costly, but God's people are called to a costly process of love that changes us.

When we are not ready for development (and development involves change) then we will have, and sadly cause, problems.

- o O o -

In the early days of the church most of the people who came were unchurched. They simple read the Bible and said 'If that's what it says then that's what we should do.'

The problems came with some of the churched people who wanted to join us.

There were those who are what I would call 'Butterfly Christians'. They flit from one flower to the next, from one church to another, always wanting to taste new things and never content to settle. They have the wrong sort of unsettledness.

The funny thing is that they think that none of the ministers know what's going on. I remember at one of our ministers fraternals when we swapped notes about who had lost who and who had gained them, someone said 'It's the migrating season again.'

Another leader added ' I've got a couple of migrants to swop. Anyone want them?'

Have you heard of the 'Oh-Oh' gift?

One Sunday, just as we were preparing for worship, a couple arrived at our baby church, looking it up and down. The 'Oh-Oh' gift started working. 'Oh, oh.' I thought.

'The Lord has told us to come here' they softly intoned.

There are some types the 'Oh-Oh' gift can tell a mile off. They go to a church, get dissatisfied with it, try to change it, and then abandon it after dropping off a load of their emotional rubbish leaving it to rot in a corner in a way that is destined to unsettle and upset others.

As they told me about their 'divine guidance' I silently prayed under my breath, 'Then, Lord, please tell them to go away again.'

Don't get me wrong. I'm not against the church helping problem people, but one of the most important questions Jesus asked was 'Do you WANT to be healed?'

Most of these people don't want to be healed, in fact at times they can become 'plants' that the devil loves to send to distract or disrupt the work of God.

Anyway, within a couple of weeks they flitted off to find a better church.

Something that John Wimber said in one of his church planting lectures was that before you can deal with all the problem people that come to your door you have to build a strong enough church community that can properly care for them.

Sometimes you have to say 'No' to very needy people in order to build up and equip a church that can help them later on.

We learned this lesson the hard way.

- o O o -

The local Roman Catholic Church was called 'The church of the Holy Family' I wanted to call our place 'The Church of the Happy Family' because we laughed such a lot together and hugged one another just like a happy family.

Agnes (not her real name) was a middle aged woman who came to us deeply hurt. She found it difficult to look at you and visibly stiffened at anything more than a formal handshake - we weren't called the hugging church for nothing!

Maybe we should have been called 'The church of the Huggy Family'.

Very courageously one day she asked for help.

Initially she was prepared to receive prayer/counselling ministry.

In the early days Heather and I did this on our own together, but as a principle we tried to get others in on the action with us, in order to train them to do the stuff.

Invariably we found that those who received healing, whether that was spiritual, physical or emotional healing, were the first ones wanting to put into practice what they had received and learned to help others.

So I and another lady in the church set aside a couple of hours each week to try to help Agnes.

Agnes had been having regular sessions with a psychiatrist when she came to us, which helped with some of the diagnosis of her problems (we would never belittle the work of any psychiatrist) but this tended to leave her like a cripple aware of her disability and maybe even its cause, but without the crutches to start walking again. She knew the problem but not how to deal with it.

Following many hours of prayer, and after she had slowly and painfully opened up her heart to the hurts and abuse that had emotionally crippled her, she began to work on with them with us. But then she came to a specific point where she was not prepared to take a particular course of action in recognition and forgiveness. She still wanted prayer but was not ready to go any further in dealing with her situation.

Sadly, despite crossing so many pain barriers she opted for an easy road and shrank back into the shadows until eventually she slipped right out of the church.

A lot of time had been given in trying to help her and in bringing her to this point. Many hours were spent on what was, in measure, helpful for her, but for us, in building a church community, a bit of a sidetrack to our primary objective of making a church strong enough to help people like her.

A church that wants to be effective needs to develop relationships built on a balanced mutual commitment of 'care and share', not on a one-way street of 'meet my needs'. There has to be a strong foundation of healthy relationships on which to build a healing community that can reach out to those who suffer from dysfunctional relationships.

- o O o -

Another way that we tried to build and develop relationships was in home groups.

After a while our house was too small for all the people wanting to come midweek.

We had them in the main room, round the corner (not the bend, I hope) of our L-shaped lounge, up the stairs, young people squashed into my small study, others in the kitchen (alright for those who wanted a crafty cup of tea). In fact people were just about everywhere.

So we decided to divide into smaller groups. We tried various methods to find the best for us.

We tried area groups with everyone of all ages going to a 'family home' where usually both Mum and Dad couldn't go out to another group together because of the kids. We attempted to have someone from the worship team to lead the worship times, someone from the pastoral team to keep an eye on pastoral needs, and someone from the teaching team to lead the Bible studies at each of these homes.

Some individuals found problems with cat allergies, or being the only young person in an area group. so we had to maintain flexibility.

Then, later, we tried interest groups. The Teaching Team prepared a number of different series of studies ranging from 'What the Cults Say', 'Family Relationships', 'Church Values', a life study on Elijah, through to a straight Bible study in the book of Nehemiah. People could then choose what track they wanted to take.

This helped to meet members needs at the point where they felt they were at, and gave lots of scope for the Teaching team to be stretched and used every week.

Then we tried rotating the members of the Teaching Team - each one taking a six week course in various homes whilst the actual groups remained static. We tried all ways.

One of these 'peripatetic' (not to be confused with a 'very pathetic') teachers writes:

'Going from group to group as part of the teaching team taught me far more than I was able to teach them.

At Denis and Carol's house we grappled with the basic tenets of the Christian Faith in a group which included new Christians and 'nearly' Christians. Even this challenge did not stretch us as much as did the serious illness of their baby daughter. As we prayed round her cot God grew our understanding. He gave us visions, words of knowledge and did miracles in her life.

At Mark and Michelle's (another young couple) the biggest impact on me was their passion for the lost. They cared for neighbours, friends, and colleagues, and used every imaginative way possible to bring them to Jesus.

The group at a third young couple's house (Simon and Lesley) led to deeper worship and intimacy in prayer. It was a spiritual oasis.

At Bob and Norah's (an older couple) with a very diverse group I was put through my paces as I tried to learn better how to include all, draw out the shy ones, curb the over-vocal, and foster acceptance of one another whilst keeping firmly on track with the Bible.

The benefit of our church set-up was that we were all free to fail, to learn and grow.

I did all three.....'

We even tried 'variety' groups. For example one group majored on Bible Teaching, while another worked on bringing in and helping to faith those who didn't yet know Jesus. Yet another group was what they called a Fun Group, where people could relax together and pray for one another.

Constantly we had to grapple with the question - What is a Home Group for? We fluctuated between, and at times struggled over, the different emphases of teaching, pastoral/fellowship, prayer, and faith sharing.

Once again change kept things on the boil, and brought different people together at different times.

As well as these midweek groups the various teams met monthly for encouragement, training, and reflection. These also created small group relationships.

- o O o -

'David is in hospital with a broken leg', 'Wan has an interview today for a new job', 'Tricia's baby died in his sleep last night', 'Hilary's car was written off on the A6 as she was going to teach in Bedford. She's suffering from shock and whiplash'.

The messages would flash from one phone to another as the prayer chain went into operation.

The Prayer Core Team had worked out a system with people who wanted to pray and had telephones to contact one another when an emergency arose. It was called either a Prayer Chain or Prayer Wheel (as the last in the chain phoned the first and we knew the request had got round OK). Often people confined to home or who couldn't be involved in other more physically active teams would wrestle in prayer on behalf of those of us who were activists in the church.

Praying for one another was a good relationship builder.

Prayer was THE most important foundation for our work.

We didn't allow people to say 'I'm afraid all I can do is pray' They were special. They could hold their heads up high in the church family and say 'My ministry in this church is prayer'.

Mind you, they had some unusual requests like 'My sister's cat is sick. Please pray for its healing' or 'It's the Three Counties cup final on Sunday morning, please pray that my son's team wins'.

Mavis, who was a new Christian, had been told about the power of the name of Jesus, so after half-time in that cup final in which her son's team was losing 4-0, every time they approached the opposition's goal she shouted, 'In the name of Jesus.' How excited she was to tell me later 'It works. They won 5-4.'

Every time they approached the opposition's goal she shouted 'In the name of Jesus'

Gently I explained that maybe that was taking an unfair advantage. However she didn't think so - as she said in her testimony the next Sunday.

The real gluttons for punishment in relationship building were those who went on holiday together. Holidays are enough to test any relationship.

We found that out when we as a church family went to Cefn Lee to the Mid Wales Christian Centre and we shared wooden cabins together. What with babies crying, adults snoring, children running in and out with muddy boots, and Wales putting on one of its famous heavenly water exhibitions (is that why the national emblem is a 'Leak'?) some came back to Luton the greater in grace (those who slept) but others a bit shorter in patience (those of us who didn't).

Some enthusiastic souls decided to go to a welsh 'chapel' service on the Sunday evening.

How different from our lively family gatherings.

The small congregation gasped as we walked in chatting to one another and laughing - men in t-shirts and some of the women in jeans!

The hymn board announced six ancient and long hymns for the organist to peddle her way through on her wheezy instrument with all the endurance of a long distance marathon runner.

The prayers, with all their 'Thee's and 'Thou's droned on like the sleepy bee that buzzed around the flowers on the communion table.

A young lay preacher, raising his Bible, laboured point after point to the stoney faced regulars.

Was there any life here? we wondered.

Then one of our folk noticed through a side window some cows in the field a few feet away from the chapel and nudged the others in the group.

The cows were looking over the hedge at the preacher and slowly nodding what seemed to be their approval of his message. Every so often they voiced a prolonged and mournful 'Mo-o-o' like a solemn 'Amen.'

We could hardly restrain our stifled giggles.

We returned to the Centre rocking with laughter.

'Some service you must have had.' the others said.

'Some service!' we replied, realising how fortunate we were to have a church family like ours despite any problems we might be facing.

A group of us also went camping regularly to the Keswick Convention in the Lake District, and 'New Wine' Holiday Week in Somerset.

Those occasions brought us together - sometimes literally - and not just when caravans managed to meet at a Service Station on the Motorway to talk about overheating engines, share some sandwiches, and have a few hours kip together in the motorway car park.

One year the main Keswick Convention tent was ripped apart in a gale. That night I went round hammering in the loose tent pegs of the less experienced on site. They slept while I secured their tents. Somehow Isaiah's words about the need to 'strengthen your stakes' has never looked quite the same since.

Another year it rained and rained. Well, it often did at Keswick - where do you think the Lakes come from? It was at Keswick that I saw my only triple rainbow.

But that year it rained. Really rained.

It rained so much that one of the Scripture Union camp sites started to flood. Tents were moved as the water crept across the field

Rachel, our youngest, and her friend Jo were persuaded to abandon their tent late one night and sleep in another tent. Just as well because next morning their tent was floating three inches deep in water. John and Jan's tent looked more impressive, a bit like a castle with a moat round it in which Martin, their young son, was trying to fish.

Difficulties bring people together. They teach us about a 'servant heart'. The spiritual spin-offs far outweigh the problems that any one person might have if there is real love between us.

We even took the young people camping to build relationships with them and between them.

Every so often we took our young people away for what we called a 'Mini-Weekend', staying in various church halls in the county.

Off we would go in cars and vans driven by volunteers and parents, loaded to the roof with food, equipment and young people raring to go. Some were apprehensive (and I don't just mean children) as it would be their first time away from their parents.

Once, one Whitsun, we braved tenting in the church grounds of Cotton End Baptist Church, which was by their ancient graveyard. Many youngsters survived their first night without going to the toilet there for fear of meeting something in the graveyard.

Those weekends brought young people and helpers together in ways that have continued through the years.

'Do you remember the water fight in swimming costumes in the rain?' 'Do you remember playing Coastguards and

Smugglers and the time Andrew skidded into the river?' 'Do you remember the meal when Martin came up for FIFTHS?' 'Do you remember when we put a wet sponge in Ryder's sleeping bag?' 'Do you remember the midnight feast his daughters arranged after he said 'No more noise' and he then fell asleep?'

'Do you remember learning about Following in the Steps of Jesus?' 'Do you remember laying tables and washing up for the first time?' 'Do you remember the prayer times we had together?' 'Do you remember someone praying before food God bless this bunch as they munch their lunch?'

'Do you remember ....?'

And do I remember the state of exhaustion Heather and I arrived home in after a weekend of non-stop activities, cooking, eating, washing up and Bible talks! Wow!

My, you have to be a survivor to be a church planter!

Chapter 7

Fittings that don't always fit

One roof truss that we had to make by hand was a real problem. It went from the top of the main roof to a corner wall at an angle of 45 degrees and across at 45 degrees. The wood was 5cm thick by 25cm deep - and, lacking electricity, we had to cut it with a handsaw.

'Oh ******* ****** not again!' exploded the voice of one of our faithful non Christian helpers way up on the roof. 'It still won't fit.'

For the third time this double-angle-cut proved to be wrong.

We spent all day on one piece of wood trying to get it right, and lost a lot of time, wood and patience in the process.

Building a 'church people' can have as many failures when we can't get the difficult angular bits to fit together snugly.

Agnes, the lady we spent hours trying to help but who in the end missed out on her healing, wasn't our only disappointment.

There was the couple who came and spent some time with us, but who after a while started rocking the boat by criticising the family services.

Coming in at an angle they stated, 'What this church needs is some deep teaching.'

Because we had the children with us all the time, and new unchurched Christians, I used to speak in simple terms using plenty of illustrations and participation, which made them think that we weren't looking at the Bible seriously.

In fact, Sunday by Sunday we had studied subjects like Discipleship, Spiritual Warfare, Covenant relationships etc. We had also gone through, chapter by chapter, whole books like Luke and Acts, and even Haggai and Daniel.

Then we had the Home Groups where people went into great depths as they unpacked some of the things we looked at on Sundays.

But I began to have my doubts. Was I really not giving 'meat'?

Another member encouraged me one week by saying 'The problem is this: they can understand what you say and they are challenged to do something about it. By deep teaching they mean something they can't understand and so don't have to do anything about it.'

But this was one of our areas of difficulty. Often it was the 'church people' who came with their 'church' hats on (sometimes literally) who brought many of their old forms and habits with them and expected to superimpose them on us.

Family worship was a case in point.

To try to avoid misunderstandings we developed what we called a TalkBack time.

Once a month after the service we spent time in prayer, sharing what we felt God might be saying, and discussing our thoughts on a variety of subjects.

Many times differences arose at our monthly Talk Backs about the children. 'They ought to be in Sunday School' one or two regularly said.

'Why?' I generally asked.

Often the problem boiled down to a selfish reason. 'I want it to be quiet.' said one.

Some genuinely had hearing difficulties like Dorothy - our OAP-er. That was different, and we struggled over it. But she, with a shrug of her shoulders after any particularly trying Sunday, would give me her wry smile, and battle on.

'I find it hard to concentrate.' said another who was constantly coo-ing at nearby babies during our services.

Another objection was 'The children need to learn at their own level', yet often parents would be surprised at how much their kids had learned on a Sunday, despite sitting under a table or wandering about at the back.

To us the children's contributions were as valid as any other.

We tried to explain this in our 'Introducing Ourselves Pack' which was an attempt to answer peoples' queries about us. 'To avoid the traditional problem of integrating children into full worship, and to obey the command 'Be my Family' we believe children should be part of today's church so that they can see, follow, and participate in all the opportunities given to adults to worship and serve the Lord'.

During our services we provided opportunity for people to share anything that they felt God might be saying. At the end of one service a grandma said 'I saw something like a bright light'. She felt a bit embarrassed as no-one else said anything. However as people collected up the Bibles and we got ready for tea one child came up and said 'During our time of quiet I saw in my mind everything all black with the words 'I want' written on it.'

'Hold it everyone. We have something else.' I shouted.

So I explained Tracey's picture. Then Tracey's Mum said 'Well, actually, I had this phrase 'Be my moths' but I felt foolish saying something like that.'

'What do moths do when they see a light?' I asked.

'They fly to it.' someone said.

We had been concerned for some time about self will, or the 'I-want' factor, in the church.

A number of people were getting more concerned about their likes and dislikes, and how they wanted the church to be. They wanted a nice church, a neat church. They wanted things to be organised 'properly' - meaning 'safely'. People were wanting to ease back from the challenge of 'living on the edge' and wanted to shelter a bit more in the 'comfort zone'.

Now we were hearing from God: God is light. We are in the darkness of self will, but the Lord is saying 'Be my moths' Come to the light.

What had unlocked it all? The word of God through a child.

Sometimes while we were worshipping we asked the children to draw something. Not colour in a Bible picture or draw Cowboys and Indians, but draw something that they felt God was giving them as part of our worship.

Many times at the end of worship not only would there be some great ideas, but many of the pictures would be similar. If God could speak to Samuel a word to shake Eli and Israel why couldn't he speak today though our children?

I must admit I had been impressed by the number of times Jesus was surrounded by children in his ministry. I often reminded myself of the time the 'religious' leaders of his day complained about the exuberance of the children. Jesus' reply was 'If they are silenced the stones will cry out' Jesus seemed to like having the children around.

Despite this, there were constant tensions about the children and we failed to keep some members because of this. However I felt strongly that we must hold on to our calling to be a family.

Heather, however, says 'I don't think we did fail to help the quieter ones. There were a number of people who had a quiet temperament who managed to adapt to a certain amount of variety. But within this variety there were many times of quiet and contemplation. And of course there was always the value of the Home Groups that took their own shapes'

I suppose that we could also say that we 'failed' those who came to us looking for a safe or traditional church.

We were actually a bit of a hotchpot as far as who came and what we did.

The church believed it was right once a month to have an Anglican style communion service - getting permission to reprint certain of the set prayers from the ASB Prayer Book.

We made a bolt together communion rail with kneeler that allowed people to come forward for communion or to receive a blessing, while everyone continued with songs of worship. We found this beneficial as people were not forced to take a plate or cup or pass it by. They could stay where they were and worship or make the choice to come out. Everyone could then be involved in communion one way or another.

As people were celebrating the new covenant of salvation they were also able to sign our church covenant, so making an agreement with the Lord, with his people, and with the work we were doing of telling others about Jesus.

Generally, however, our services were open for more participation. Like the time we had a polo race. Everyone was put into a team and given a straw to put in their mouth. The first person in each team had a polo put on their straw which they had to pass on without handling it to the next straw in their team and so on to the end.

Great cheers rose from the winning team, and the next, until finally a groan rumbled out from the last. This changed to an eruption of moans from the rest when the last team were all given prizes.

'It's not fair,' grumbled not only the children in the winning team but some of the adults, 'we were first'.

'I never said the first ones would get anything.' I stated. 'But what I'm illustrating is something called GRACE, and how Jesus said that the first will be last and the last first.'

On other occasions we would break up into groups for activities, discussions, or for prayer.

When we worshipped we allowed people to be themselves. If they wanted to stand, to sit, to kneel, sing in English or an unknown tongue, to raise their hands, clap them, clasp them, sing or be silent, open their eyes or close them, whatever was real in their heart before the Lord Jesus was okay.

Some people found that very threatening. One lady said 'I don't know what to do or who to copy'. Yes, there is insecurity in difference, but maybe that shows if our security is in a group dynamic or in the Lord.

We allowed people to be themselves

In this way we demonstrated in practice one of our values - the value of the individual and their relationship with the Lord[8]

Sadly, because of this sense of insecurity we lost some other people.

- o O o -

---

(8) See Appendix 1 No. 4

Often though, what seem failures and losses to us can be very different when seen in the light of building the Kingdom of God.

Every year we had an official deputation from our local Baptist Association to vet us about further funding, so we were always on our best behaviour when they came.

All the leaders from the different teams had come for a time of prayer and worship with them and were given an opportunity to explain what their teams had been up to over the year. It was great hearing what God had been doing in them personally and with others they were working with.

Some of our people were very self conscious, they were not used to being looked on as leaders of a church. Over the months in Luton we had tried to build a different model of leadership based on function not position, with those who were more concerned about serving than about an office or role.[9]

What excited me about our bunch was that they had wonderful servant hearts.

When our visitors asked about our 'church structures' we explained that we enjoyed a very fluid and flexible form of life together.

This did not appeal to one of our 'visitors' - a deacon of long standing who I felt enjoyed his title more than the task. With a somewhat belittling manner he talked about the need for trust deeds, constitutions, church officers etc. and finally added something about 'When you have a proper church with good deacon material.....'.

Having had some sad experiences of what I came to call 'demons meetings', because they stemmed from more power struggles than spiritual concerns, I admit that I 'rose' to his remark and said that I much preferred our type of leaders because they were humble and had servant hearts.

- o O o -

Anne was a case in point.

She came to us as a wounded, and unsettled person after a 'quick fix' prayer in another church that hadn't worked. She

(9) See Appendix 5

had been told that she would never do anything for the Lord.

Sadly the other church had not really helped her to face her problems. 'Just believe and you will be healed' was their approach. But her problem wasn't an Elastoplast job. She went through a lot of prayer with us, discovering the patient healing love of the Lord, and then joined our prayer ministry team.

However she always preferred to let others take a lead and liked to take a back seat. None the less it was evident that she had a really caring heart and after a lot of prayer eventually joined the pastoral team.

The pastoral team unanimously recognised her gifting, and saw also a leadership gifting in her. So they told her that they felt that the Lord wanted her to lead the pastoral team. She did this wonderfully, though very quietly. She was an ideal pastoral person.

She worked at the local hospital in administration. When reorganization was happening and her job there was under threat we seriously wondered about the possibility of her becoming a paid part time worker. Unfortunately our church grant would have been lost if we had, and anyway the hospital kept her on.

As a single lady, at times she found our church a bit overwhelmingly 'family' orientated. This was another of our 'failure' areas. There were other singles who, when they came to us, found being a church family, and being surrounded by so many families, hard. We tried all we could to include them, though one or two then felt that they were being patronised.

We wrestled with the problems of those who were single, divorced, and bereaved. We thought about a specific group for them, but felt that such a group would merely marginalise them and reinforce a sense of exclusion.

We tried to form links between those on their own and families who could support them and that they in turn could offer support to.

After much prayer and many attempts we still felt that we were failing a number of these people.

However we believed that we had to hold on to the vision the Lord gave us to be a family, or else we would be failing the Lord.

Many churches have problems because they have an identity crisis - they don't know what they are or should be. We knew what we should be but that meant that those that couldn't accept this were bound to feel uncomfortable.

Also having a slight hearing problem Anne found the constant background noise of active children and vocal babies hard to cope with. She battled on, and the Lord did some tremendous things for her, and through her.

Eventually after many discussions together and further prayer with us we accepted the fact that a new Anglican church on the next estate was more conducive for her and the right step for her to take. Sadly she left us - with no ill feelings - and went there.

What was to us a loss has become their gain as now she is a full member of staff working - yes, you've guessed it - as the church pastoral worker.

- o O o -

They came to us exhausted, physically, emotionally, and spiritually.

Sue and Peter had been working for the Salvation Army, and had been quite important to a local Corps., but they were wrung out.

They moved onto our estate and as usual I visited them in their first week. No way was I wanting to pinch people from another church. Our purpose wasn't to build a church with stolen sheep. However, they rather guiltily expressed their desire to come to our home for our midweek prayer-time.

I assured them that it was alright for them to be able to receive as well as to give. 'Look on it as a bit of hospitalization' I said ' You know that you aren't forsaking the Army just having a break to recuperate.'

They came to us eventually Sundays (as we met in the afternoons and their Corps. in the mornings) and midweek for about nine months.

During that time they were refreshed and renewed. Eventually they returned to their Corps. with a greater sense of the Lord's calling and power on them.

It wasn't that Peter and Sue were fittings that didn't fit. They were 'temporary fittings' like some others who came to us. Sometimes it was right for our church to act as a bolt hole for people whose churches didn't give space for a rest.

To avoid such dangers, this was one of the reasons that we decided to review all gifts and ministries in the church annually. Then if someone felt after trying one form of service for a year that this wasn't for them, or if they had been serving for some time and needed a year out, no-one felt guilty or could be made to feel like that if they had 'time out'.

Sadly a number of churches grab every new member that enters the doors and force them into the present need - i.e. Sunday School teacher, Boy's Brigade helper, tea rota - irrespective of their gifting, and then hold them there till they drop, die or disappear out the back door.

It's amazing how many exhausted and guilty Christians there are in the churches, and even sadder how many aren't!

Genèrally for anyone who considered coming to us or staying past convalescence my frequent comment was ' If the Lord wants you here, stay. But if he doesn't, we don't want you here. Remember what happened to the ship with Jonah on board. We can do without storms because of disobedient fugitives.'

A basic understanding of some of these things is needed right at the beginning of starting a church. Workable principles need to be understood and acted on right from the beginning, though people must be able to distinguish between Principles (which are non negotiable) and Practices (which are subject to change as situations alter).

If these are not sorted out early on a church can end up like some prewar homes I've visited where modern fittings have been tried throughout the years but have turned out not to be right.

All you end up with is a house with walls full of holes. Holey, as opposed to holy!

Chapter 8

Windows and Doors

The shell of the church property had been open for anyone to enter for some time. Dogs wandered in and out, delighted children played and swung in the rafters (despite warning signs), and one tramp had used it as his overnight accommodation and toilet - yuk. It was time to make the property secure.

'We need as many people as possible to come together on Saturday so that we can close the place up,' went the announcement.

We had 19 windows with 53 sealed units of glass to fix, 6 doors with 12 more sealed units to install, and the main doors to hang with 24 bits of long narrow glass (all slightly different) to get right.

We started at 6.00am and continued to work throughout the day with only a couple of brief pauses for refreshments.

Nine workers came during that day (two from a nearby church who hung the main entrance doors) to sort, pin, and putty in all those double-glazed units that I had managed to purchase at a special price from a local window firm.

It was ten thirty at night when, by the light (or headlights) of a Mini, we wearily puttied in the final window.

The main doors had been fixed and temporary glass put in, but four of the six other doors had to have chipboard quickly pinned in place before we left for a good bath and night's sleep.

We wanted lots of glass in the church (which incidentally only got broken once) because of a principle.

On the one hand we wanted people outside to see us inside praising and serving our Lord.

Many churches appear to be 'secret societies' locked away behind huge dark doors. Even if those are open you have to then go into a closed cupboard called a vestibule, and through some more wooden doors into the unknown.

So first of all we wanted everything to be open and above board. We wanted people to be able to look in and see what was going on.

Secondly, we wanted to be able to see out, to be aware of

the world about us. Though that was a bit of a distraction when the Pub put on an 'It's a Knockout' in our shared car park one Sunday. I could see our people during the service nudging one another and straining to see the teams outside falling over the different obstacles.

Churches that are inward looking, seeing only their own needs and being oblivious of the world outside are forgetting their primary purpose - to win the world for Jesus. Eventually they become as neurotic as a teenager looking at his own face in the mirror and worrying about the spots that blemish his self image.

..they become as neurotic as a teenager looking at his own face in the mirror...

Windows and doors speak a message.

We wanted to show that we were a part of the community not apart from it.

The week we fixed the windows I had a phone call from the police. They wanted to visit. Wow, how conscience works overtime on occasions like that. However, all they wanted was to ask if they could use our building for a week. They needed to keep an eye on Sainsbury's next door which was experiencing some petty crime in its car park at night. So two lonely policemen, with their radios twittering away, perched all night like owls on a temporary chipboard floor we put up, popping their heads out of our skylight windows.

Already we were becoming a church in the community, for the community.

But how did these things develop?[10]

First. It started with lots of visiting. Then there were the meetings in our house every Sunday for tea and a family service.

Next, we began our children's club for those who came on a Sunday. This developed from a 'party of light' that we called a Rainbow Party to provide an alternative to the invitations many of them had been having to attend Halloween parties. Rainbow Club every Friday in our house became the time for fun and games and the opportunity for the youngsters to apply the Sunday messages to their own lives.

After this we started a Monday night prayer and Bible study evening for the adults. 'Why should only the children have a time to relax and study the Bible?' people asked.

On Monday nights we built deeper relationships with one another.

Within less than three months we realised that something else was missing. This was put right when we had our first communion service. Communion was a great opportunity to focus on the cross. We were able to explain about, and celebrate, the love of the Lord Jesus when he gave his life for the mess we all make of our lives, and his power that was big enough to come alive again three days later. Talking about the agreement he made with us (or covenant) became the basis later on for forming covenant relationships with one another.

The same week we had our first communion Heather started her pilot group to help people who were not as yet Christians to find out about the Lord.

The 'house groups' developed and multiplied until we had about six different groups a week.

Foundational to everything that we were doing was the need to be constantly sharing Jesus with as many people possible by every means possible.

---

(10) See Appendix 6

But this was all focused inward. We needed more light to shine out, so we made plans to let Jesus be seen more on our patch.

- o O o -

Lou Lewis has the ability to get you right where it hurts.

She is Christian singer/songwriter who trained at Dartington College of Arts in Devon and later at the Royal College of Music, has sung at many gigs, spoken at conferences, and been on TV.

As a student she tripped out on LSD, later found Jesus, and has been serving him with music ever since.

We first heard her at a national leaders conference in 1984 at Brean Sands. What she said rang a cord in our own hearts as she sang about Jesus understanding our pains. 'Don't hide away.' she sang 'Let the Lord know, then you can know yourself.'[11]

Lou and Steve became special friends to us over the years, so we invited them to Luton for a weekend of music ministry in our house where our church family were meeting (as we weren't in the church as yet). She ministered in some of the Luton and district churches.

The Lord gives Lou songs, and insights into people lives, that through tears and prayer bring healing. So it was not strange that when she finished her evening in our front room the only applause she got was silence broken by a stifled sniffle here and there.

She later used our bedroom to pray with a couple of young Mums who she sensed in her spirit (and hit the nail right on the head) had suffered abuse, as she herself had as a child.

Lou came again to Luton when our church building was eventually opened a year and a half after I had originally, and somewhat simplistically, anticipated that our DIY property would have been built.

- o O o -

Sporting a Stetson, clicking down our path in his high heeled cowboy boots, with his guitar in his hand in its hard black case,

---

(11) From the Cassette 'Don't Hide Away' - Zimrah Music

Gus arrived. Just what I anticipated a Country and Western singer to look like. However Gus's back pocket packed not a revolver but a Bible.

'Next weekend we are having a Country and Western singer/song writer coming to our home. Would you like to come?' we asked as many people as possible.

One of our neighbours, an ex-banker, loved C & W, so he quickly said 'yes' despite me warning him that Gus was a Christian who would tell his story between songs.

Gus Eyre had come down from the north of England at the invitation of another church in the area. They felt that it was right to 'tithe' some of Gus's time by loaning him out to us, as a new work, at their own expense.

We were very grateful.

The neighbours were delighted, and afterwards asked many questions about his music and faith.

Some years later he came again. This time the pub had been built and when I asked if a Christian Country and Western singer could have a live spot in the pub, the proprietors happily gave us a section of the main lounge for Gus to sing at the tables. In fact one person in the pub gave her life to Jesus because of that visit.

We got on well with the pub landlords, whom I had welcomed the day they had arrived on the estate. When we were building our own church home and needed water for mixing cement they let us take their water by hose 100yards across the car park and fill our water tanks each day.

Some folks however wondered what we were pumping in to our church.

Even though, generally, builders in their work clothes were not welcome (there were 100's of them working on the Bramingham development) I was always given a big hand when I wandered into the Lounge Bar in my tatty trousers and pullover, especially when I left my muddy boots at the door.

With such events we tried to create like a bridge in our programme with two special happenings each year on which to suspend our normal evangelistic work.

One year was typical - or untypical depending on how you look at it.

In the Spring we had what we billed a 'Magical Weekend' and invited Henry Smith. Henry was secretary of the Christian Conjurers Fellowship (UK) and a writer of Christian magical articles in a secular worldwide Magic/Conjuring Magazine. He was asked to do a Saturday evening show, and then speak on Sunday at 'a service with a difference'.

The church was packed to capacity with enthusiastic families, who enjoyed the evening and found out about the good news of Jesus. Magic!!

One little 3 year old lad who stood at the back in the arms of his grandma was so fascinated that he started to learn to do magic and has put on a few shows with his gran as a result. She became one of the leaders of our prayer ministry team - that's not about magical deception. That's God.

That same year, in the Autumn, we had a soiree.

All day a team prepared food for a full three course sit down meal for 60 guests. The church was transformed with small tables and chairs into an intimate candlelit setting. Then following the after-meal mints the Kensington Chorale from London put on a full concert of classical, light and Christian music (complete in evening dress). The second half was interspersed by the singers telling their stories of faith.

What a contrast - Conjuring and a Classical Concert!

Then there were extra 'specials' like the estate family Fun Day.

The church was grassed round with a huge lawn, most of which we had laid turf by turf, two weeks before the first wedding in the church. This happened to be for our youngest daughter and the boy next door (but two) The local rag did a page spread about 'neighbours in love', 'vicars daughter' (as I both did the ceremony and gave her away), 'builders of their own church' etc. But laying those turfs was backbreaking (as was the twice-a-day, morning and evening, summer watering).

Anyway, back to the Fun Day. We set up side shows, games, competitions, 'chuck-a-wet-sponge-at-the-dry-preacher' (did they love it and did I get wet), crockery smashing booth etc. Refreshments were served all day. But the climax for us was when the young people in our Arts Team every half hour put on a puppet show and dance presentations about the Christian message.

Earlier that morning we went round the estate in fancy dress, singing, dancing, shouting, and doing mad things while inviting people to the Fun Day.

Bonfire night was another opportunity to build bridges. We arranged a BarBQ and Bonfire, eventually serving over 300 with edible bangers, and then put on a safe firework display for everyone.

Windows let light in and let light out. But light at times can be painful as well as pleasurable, especially when the light unexpectedly catches people out in the dark.

This happened when the issue of Sunday Trading cropped up.

Our estate was a hive of activity every day of the week, but Sunday was a respite. The builders were resting, and Sainsbury's was closed. Apart from the Jehovah's Witnesses who arrived every Sunday morning by the car load, and friends visiting one another, Sunday was a day of rest. It was the one day when everyone, many of whom commuted to and from London from Monday to Friday, did their gardens, cleaned the house and car, and put out the week's washing. Even the church (us) didn't have a Sunday morning service.

By the way, we were naughty about the Jehovah's Witnesses. Those of us on the evangelistic team often sussed out where they were going next.

As we had an afternoon service we decided to go out door to door visiting in the morning just before, and often just where, the JW's were going that day.

'No we are not Jehovah's Witnesses', we replied after the house owners' question 'Who are YOU?. One of THEM?'

'We are from your friendly 'local' over by the pub and Sainsbury's. If you have a few minutes we would like to tell you about who we are and what we believe.' Most had time to listen to what we had found in Jesus, and often asked how we differed from the JWs'

As a result of the confusion the JW's created we produced a little leaflet called 'Guarantee' about nine thing Christian are guaranteed that the Jehovah's Witnesses lack.[12]

---

(12) See Appendix 7

Anyway, as I said, generally Sunday was peaceful and quiet. But then ... WAR. Stores throughout Great Britain decided to break the Law and open up on the three Sundays before Christmas.

What were we do? We had a good relationship with our local Sainsbury's management, in fact when they wanted to build a Petrol Station in their Car Park, to lessen the inconvenience to them we allowed them to put a lot of their equipment on our grounds.

After prayer we believed that we should make a visible statement of conscience, to let the light shine.

So, first I went to see the manager personally and explained that as Christians we felt that people should obey both the law of God and nation. He explained that he had to obey his directive from head office. So we warned him that as a result we would be making a peaceful protest with placards outside on the road by their entrance.

When Sunday arrived a bunch of church members met at the church to pray and then pick up their placards. Under a Manger Scene our posters asked the Christmas shoppers 'Whose day, anyway?' As customers arrived to do their shopping, with a smile we gave them a leaflet that encouraged them for the sake of health, conscience, and family well-being (as some of our members were now being obliged to work on a Sunday also) to obey the Law of God and Country.

Some people turned away seeing our placards and went back home. Some folks passing by on the way to their morning services gave us a hoot and a big wave. But some irate drivers on the way in to Salisbury actually swerved trying to drive AT us even though we were not obstructing their entrance.

We felt that this was because the issue was not just an economic thing but a spiritual one.

The papers took the story up, and plastered us across the front page.

We did wondered though if we had spoilt the goodwill we enjoyed on the estate by this protest and whether the Midnight Christmas Eve service in a few days time would suffer, but it was as full as ever for our Candlelight Service.

As the light of the candles shone out of the windows of our

church that Christmas we prayed that in some way the light we were trying to bring to the estate and nation would also shine out and show people the way to the child king we were trying to follow.

The light of God's love that we were trying to show to our estate by becoming its heart and its conscience was not only to be comforting but was also to be challenging.

The light the Lord wanted to shine through our windows that particular Christmas had to be prophetic.

Chapter 9

Power Points

After Ray had dug yet another trench with his bright yellow digger - this time the length of Sainsbury's car park as the gas and electricity had to come in one end and the water the other - I stood there up to my knees in the chalky gully he had made asking in my typically ignorant way 'Which colour pipe is for what?'

I knew that brown pipes were for the drains because we had laid them earlier, but what were the yellow, blue, grey, and black ducts for?

'Yellow is for gas, black ducting for water, grey for telephone lines, and blue for electricity cables to go through' said our patient architect neighbour, David.

'Why isn't the WATER blue?' I asked, 'That's more logical?'

'The blue goes inside the black ducting', he answered patiently.

'But when you dig it up you can't see that', I groaned.

'Well that's how it is', chuckled David.

And so. one by one, the different Boards connected up the water (no more hoses from the Pub), electricity (no more cables trailing across the road to the newsagents) and eventually the gas and telephone.

How excited I was when the Eastern Electricity switched on our temporary supply - one cable, one connection, and one permissible plug. But that was all we needed to get power.

The church property wasn't actually finished for our first wedding - the marriage of our youngest daughter, Rachel, to the boy next door (but two) our electrician/security systems installer, Paul.

Two pairs of doors had chipboard tacked in instead of glass (they look beautiful in the wedding photos) and the evening before the wedding, late, saw the couple's two fathers putting the last bit of lino down in the kitchen!

As guests arrived for the service they were told 'Don't switch on the lights in the loos or our one 13amp fuse that safeguards the supply for the lights in the church, the musical instruments and amplification, and power for the tape recorder up in the roof belting out a carillon of bells, will blow'.

Little did the Electricity Board know that everything in the church would run from that one 13amp plug.

If all roads lead to Rome, for us all wires ran to that one plug.

That was a bit like our church family.

All the life of our growing church flowed from one connection - Jesus. He supplied the power of his Spirit to every activity and to everyone of us.

There was plenty of power, but we had to beware of not overloading any one person so that the fuse blew. So we shared out as much as possible to spread the load.

This showed itself particularly on a Sunday.

Let Heather give you a bird's eye view....

Nothing was ever certain or the same, hence the overworked word 'sometimes'.

- o O o -

'It's Sunday at 3.00pm, and the Worship Group are tuning up their instruments - guitars, flutes, drums, and trumpet - to the synthesizer, secreting glasses of water for later, checking music sheets from the time of prayer and preparation two days before, and touching up slightly blurred words on the acetates for the songs.

Meanwhile cups and saucers are clattering into place in the kitchen, the bar is being wiped down in readiness for all the goodies which will arrive, and the boiler is being filled and switched on low for later.

More people arrive and stand round chatting.

Some of the prayer ministry team, with any others who want to join them, are praying in the room called the Chapel, asking God about what he wants to do especially during any time of ministry at the end of the service.

Always early Yvonne arrives, with Bob pushing Mandy their youngest daughter in her wheelchair, laden with succulent sandwiches or a naughty desert, or both.

Little by little other foods arrive until the bar is full and needs to be covered over in case tiny fingers find the temptation too much.

....laden with succulent sandwiches or a naughty desert, or both.

We often provided Marmite or chocolate sandwiches, which proved very popular, especially after Bob brought a newspaper clipping one week claiming that both Marmite and Chocolate are 'Aphrodisiacs' This caused much hilarity and called for some explanation.

Although we have a rota so that everyone can have a turn at serving (the children have to serve the 'olds' first to teach servanthood) and do the washing up we never have a rota for food. People bring WHAT they want, WHEN they want, and it doesn't matter if people come empty handed. We never have too little. Sometimes we have too much, which means that those with children, or living alone, can take some treats home with them.

Gradually the room fills up with people, young and old all together for our weekly family service, and those praying come in from the chapel.

Stilling the general hubbub of excited chatter someone from the secretarial team makes a few announcements or puts them up on the screen for all to see.

Robin might stand up and ask people on the practical team to come on Saturday and help with some new work or repairs to the church, or help cut the grass.

No one, young or old escapes being sung to on their birthday. Sometimes 'Happy Birthday' is sung 5 or 6 times - there are so many!

Generally the notices, or News Time, would be right at the start, or at the end so as not to disturb the flow of worship.

Nothing is set in concrete, so the form of the service varies each week as does the seating arrangements and those taking part.

As soon as all the notices are out the way a time of praise and worship starts led by John the worship leader. This may start with the reading of a part of the Bible or a prayer, followed by four or five songs or hymns which follow on from one another so that we can really focus on God.

Either standing, sitting or kneeling this time of worship can be followed by a time of silent prayer, or the Lord's prayer, or a open time of spontaneous prayer.

Sometimes there is a special opportunity for people to tell what God has done for them, or bring requests for prayer.

Maybe Diane, the Prayer Core leader pops up to focus us on some specific prayer needs that have come up during the week on the telephone prayer chain or at a meeting for prayer that the intercessory team have had.

Maybe Anne from the Pastoral Team will ask prayer for some of the people the team visited during the past week.

On occasions we break up into 2's or 3's to pray, children and all.

This may be followed by a drama or worship dance that the Arts Team have prayerfully felt led to bring or perhaps we have a quiz. Maybe there is a slot by some of the evangelism team on Mission at home or abroad.

After this generally there is a time of life related Bible teaching by one or more of the teaching team illustrated by pictures on the screen, or an instant drama (using not just the children) or maybe an illustrative game, or a handout.

Often what is taught on a Sunday in a basic and clear manner will be teased out in more detail by the teaching team during the week in the home groups and the youth groups - but not always.

Then there is some kind of challenge or application - many times involving the prayer ministry team who in two's or three's pray for the Holy Spirit's release, healing, encouragements. and power for those who respond. This happens generally before, after, or during a further time of worship when once again the songs and musical instruments help us to focus on what we have learned and how to respond to it.

Sometimes people share a picture or word that has come into their hearts and the children will explain a picture they have been given and been inspired to draw.

Once a month we walk out to the front to eat and drink some ordinary bread and wine bought from Sainsbury's as we remember the Lords death and resurrection. Joyfully we declare ' Christ has died, Christ has Risen, Christ will come again'. Different members of the congregation help serve the bread and wine while those wanting just a blessing for themselves or their children come and are prayed for by the prayer ministry team.

Generally at the end of each service we join hands to sing or say that prayer called 'The Grace' as found in 2 Corinthians 13 v14, before everyone starts chatting together.

Anyone that wants more specific and ongoing prayer may continue where they are or go into the chapel.

Those that are on duty get busy behind the bar pouring out the teas and everyone does their best to see that visitors are well looked after and made to feel at home. If it's their first time they are asked to sign the visitors book so that the secretarial team can send them a letter of welcome and a pack about the church family.

Regulars who haven't done so on arrival pop their gifts of money into the wooden box lovingly carved by Jack, one of the practical team, that is attached to the wall by the Bibles.

After a space some of the Finance team disappear into the office to count and record the thank-you gifts in the box, and one of the team who lives by the bank will take the money off and put it in the church account next day.

Noise levels start to rise with the chatter of voices, clatter of plates, clapping and cheering as someone drops one, and a crash as one of the youngsters tries out the drums. But this is what being a family is all about.

As soon as their food is stuffed down the children dash out into the church garden to start a spontaneous game of football or 'catch me'.

After tea people leave in little groups, as one and another offer lifts home to those who need it. The pastoral team see that no one gets left out.

And hugs all round.

Once a month we get together after tea for a TalkBack time - a sort of church business meeting - and on another occasion for an informal time of quiet and communion in the chapel.

When it's all over the practical team and any volunteers sort out the rooms, stacking up the chairs and tables, vacuum the carpets, and set out the rooms ready for the Monday morning Playgroup'.

o - O - o

Of course Sunday was only one day - a sort of composite snapshot of all the other days put together.

Like none of us want electricity for only one day a week, so Sunday was not our main focus. We wanted God's power for every day of the week. For that we had Home Groups, Team meetings for training, prayer and preparation and other activities.

A church is only as strong as each of its members are, not its leader. So we, as temporary leaders, set the pattern by constantly giving away, and passing on the power for living that the Lord was giving us. In that way we could receive from others as much as we could give.

'Oooh' warned one other minister in our local Minister's Fraternal when I said how I allowed people to minister to me at the point of my weakness as much as I ministered to them, 'Oooh' he repeated ' You'll lose their respect if they see you as a weak person.'

I felt just the opposite. Maybe that's what Paul in the Bible was on about when he said 'When I'm weak then I am strong, because at that point the power of Christ can flow into and through me.'

That's the power I wanted for myself and the church family

God had given us.

The proof was when we left, as without a hiccough the church carried on the next week just as though we were, or weren't, there.

They were plugged in to the power socket without us.

Chapter 10

Extension Work

I'd always wanted to have a go with a proper crane. I suppose it came from my childhood days on Southend pier, working those slot machines with a crane inside that grabs a gift, (which invariably would slip out of its grasp). To sit there in the cab and grab things for real, and swing them around in the sky - wow!

But it was not to be.

However the next best thing to working a crane is to be in charge of it.

Early one Saturday a large lorry arrived with a huge telescopic arm that was to pick up and place our roof trusses on top of the walls that Gary and his team had now built.

Plans in hand, I carefully measured and marked out with my big pencil where on the wall plate the first one was to be put, and checked it was right. Then I measured the next... and the next... and the next.

The driver swung his seat round in his cab, and extended the crane arm to where the fork lift truck, that we had prayed for earlier when unloading, had put the trusses.

Up, up and away. The first 'A' shaped truss hung and swung there way up above us in the clear blue early morning sky, hovering like a sparrow-hawk looking for something on the ground to eat.

As it slowly descended up on the scaffolding we grabbed both ends and, as carefully as possible, set this wobbly giant on its prepared marks.

One by one we fastened together each truss in its appropriate place with odds and ends of strapping wood. But by the time we had nailed down the final one something just didn't look right. And sure enough, the smaller trusses that were to go at right angles to these main ones and overhang the end wall by 40cm only just reached the end wall!

It turned out that by a margin of 2cm here, and 1cm there, after setting out some 20 trusses, we ended up by losing nearly 30 cm.

Everything had to re-adjusted to get it exactly right this time.

This was something else that we learned the hard way. What you do at the beginning effects where you end up.

Similarly the things that we were doing in the life of our church family at the start, and at each stage along the way, set the direction for what we would to do later.

- o O o -

'I hate filling in questionnaires.' said someone as we set about finding out where our church family had come from and where we were going to.

'I love them.' I replied 'It's fun thinking of original answers to fill in'. I always did have a perverse sense of humour!

I was thinking about the National Census Form that I had filled in earlier which asked things like: Marital Status? To which I answered - Very Good!! Job Description? That was an opportunity for explaining the gospel in minuscular writing within the small square provided.

Our questionnaire showed that 80% of the church were convinced that the primary purpose of the church was evangelism - that is telling people about Jesus - and consequently over 66% expected the church to grow during the following five years.

Besides our regular door-to-door visiting, and special efforts like the concerts we put on, we also tried unusual things - like an evangelistic polling station.

- o O o -

An official brown envelope, bearing the crest of the Luton Borough Council, floated down onto the door mat.

I am dubious about brown envelopes with transparent windows on principle. They usually contain bills, or try to sell you double glazing.

Inside this one. however, was a request to use our newly opened church building, right in the centre of our estate, for the up coming election as a polling station.

The offer of money was tempting, but more important to us was the thought that we would be getting at least 3000 residents coming in through the doors.

The leaders prayed about this request and felt it was right to allow the property to be used as a polling station, but with a rider (no, nothing to do with me) . We stated that we wished to use the entrance foyer as a place to provide refreshments.

The Council speedily replied giving us the all clear but with their own proviso. Yes, they said, the church entrance could be used for serving refreshments, as long as there was no politicing that went on there.

The entrance of our church was purpose built to be user friendly. You came in through double Windsor doors - the sort with lots of vertical strips of glass. Facing you was an open bar kitchen the other side of this large entrance area (about 5mx9m) that could easily seat 70 people round neat circular tables. Remember our church life was based on Sunday worship followed by tea together.

So we did the tables out with white cloths, menus, etc., and from 7.00am were ready to provide breakfasts, lunches, and suppers, and throughout the day sandwiches, cakes, coffee and biscuits.

The borough officials arrived early and put up their large black and white signs with fingers pointing to the main hall where they had erected their booths and set up their tables. We added a large poster that we placed just inside the front door showing a large rosette with a line slashed through it. Above the rosette bold words stated 'This is a politics free zone' It was just as well, as at one point one of the candidates came in for coffee, ready to do battle, and had to be gently pointed to the poster.

One of the candidates...had to be gently pointed to the poster

'This is a rare occasion when we can talk about religion, but not politics.' I joked with him.

That day about 150 people stopped off for refreshments of one sort or another and chatted about the church and the Christian faith. Some took booklets about what we believed.

One man said 'I've always wanted to come in and see what goes on here, but was afraid to. I think it's great here.'

Others started coming to the church as a result of entering an evangelistic polling station.

Apparently the council staff have voted our church top of their list of popular polling venues as it is warm (thanks to Alf's plumbing), welcoming, and always has refreshments on the go.

Although there were many similar unusual things that we attempted in order to fulfil our aim 'to know Jesus and make him known', two activities set major directions for the extension of the work and life of the church.

- o O o -

Some of us had been asking the question: 'What does ministry to the poor mean for us on Bramingham Park?' This was a difficult question to answer on our affluent estate.

There were no 'poor' on our development. Most people drove the few hundred yards to Sainbury's in cars flashing the latest registration plates. You couldn't easily get a mortgage to move here unless both partners were at work, or one just about killed himself/herself in the attempt.

In fact when we considered moving to Bramingham I felt distinctly uncomfortable thinking that everyone was socially way above me, and I'd do better on the council estate next door.

It didn't help when my Mum decided to lash out on her 70th birthday by buying a brand new 'gold' Opel Manta sports for herself (at previous churches she was known as 'SuperGran' because of all the sports cars she drove)! At the same time as lashing out on herself she decided to present me with my own birthday present - the latest Vauxhall Astra estate. 'When I die why should the tax man have my hard earned cash?' was her only comment. At the time I felt acutely embarrassed having existed as a clergyman with old cars that like a rabbit quickly ran to ground at the slightest noise.

Well, back to the poverty issue, as a church we needed to work out something applicable to this aspect of our 'social conscience'.

The answer came in at an angle with a personal idea and question that Jan presented me with.

Jan, besides being part of our prayer ministry team, was a home tutor, and responsible for Home Tuition for the Luton area.

She taught children, one on one, who were stuck at home due to prolonged sickness, school girls who were pregnant or had babies, and a group given the name 'school-phobics' (I wish I'd heard about that when I was at school).

Problems were encountered when Jan arrived at homes that were not conducive to teaching (too much noise from the TV, inquisitive pets, interfering smaller brothers and sisters etc.) or, after travelling some miles by car, having the frustration of sometimes finding that the family had gone out shopping or simply didn't answer the door!

The biggest problem however was lack of tutors in the area. How could so few help so many?

After a time of prayer about her concerns, she told me how she had this idea/vision.

'If we could get a few children together in a relaxed setting, we could cover more needs, and through children working together get some of the school-phobics on the way back into schooling. What would be the possibility of using our newly opened church?' she wanted to know.

Already we had links with schools through Jan's husband John who taught at Warden Hill School, and with a 'special needs' school called Five Springs on the next estate through Titia, one of our members and a teacher there.

When Five Springs lacked a music teacher (which was often) Heather popped over there and played for assemblies and one or two 'open days'. Through that link I ended up taking their Easter Services each year. One year we took our two daughters over with their musical instruments to play and sing. Then with a bit of conjuring to illustrate the Easter story, we explained that Jesus really did care for all of them, even if other people in the area were unkind.

In fact, before we were really up and running in our property, three years after beginning our friendship, the Five Springs school marched across from Marsh Farm to Bramingham and into our hardly ready church for their Easter service.

Before we left Luton the woodwork teacher presented the church with an adjustable oak lectern in gratitude.

But, regular, five days a week Home tuition in our church property was another matter!

However, as usual, the church family prayed about it, and quickly came to believe that this was something that God wanted us to be involved with. So Jan was given the green light to start with her friend and colleague Jenny and some other Home Tutors, what was to become a rather novel means of teaching.

One problem that cropped up was the need to care for babies for the 14/15 year old (or maybe younger) Mums who came and some of the tutors' or helpers' toddlers.

Pauline, one of our church members, felt that the Lord wanted her to do some child minding, so she offered to help with the babies.

This child-minding service became the precursor for a full-time creche, play group, and group for first time mums with a Health Stop, called No 1 (but more about that later).

The problem was that Pauline was in Heather's Tuesday Young Mums (in their 20's/30's) Group in our home.

The most sensible solution was to move this group over from our house and into the church, as they already had a pre-installed baby minder - me.

So it was that the apostle/church planter/church building foreman and odd-job man/pastor/etc., ended up playing with two young children, two toddlers, and three babies. That meant building with play bricks, being a rocking horse, cuddling crying babies. finding lost dummies and wiping snotty noses.

Does 'all things to all men' include all things to all babies?

The spin-off from looking after these little 'uns was that at Family Services I had few problem with the children. They looked on me as the man to play games with. Often they would wander over and give me a hug round the knees mid service. I remember serving communion one handed one Sunday, as in the other a small child was fast asleep in my arm, having climbed up for a cuddle earlier in the service.

Many other Christian opportunities came through this Home Tuition activity, like praying for and seeing at least one child healed physically, and another emotionally, as well as having good times with the Tutors and some of the parents.

Jan's vision came to a crossroads when the County Council said that they had no more funds for Home Tutoring, and started to lay off teachers. That brought things to a painful junction.

With Jan we wrestled with the question: 'If this Home Tuition project really was of God how would it continue?'

After lots more prayer - the sort that says simply 'What now, Lord?' - the church encouraged Jan to 'go independent'. As a church we agreed that initially we would help this project by not charging anything for using the church - not only because Jan was losing her secure wages, but because we felt that what she was doing was part of the church's vision also.

So Jan wrote to schools with a pamphlet explaining about the Centre's Educational Services, and Creche. asking them to invest in the scheme, by sending their Home Tuition students to us. It was around this period that schools were beginning to look after their own budgets, and could place students where they wished.

It was also at this time that she applied to the Universities' Examinations Board authorities to register Bramingham Park as a proper examination centre.

After we left Luton and went to work in Albania the Home Tuition Centre took a new turn, registering as a small non-profit making 'Small Business Company' to ensure that there were no legal loopholes through which the work could be undermined by the strong opposition of the L.E.A.

Throughout all their difficulties Jan and her team continually prayed about their work and bit by bit the struggles were overcome and the opposition dispersed.

Six days a week they now occupy the, at last, completed upstairs.

The church has also branched out educationally under its new minister Lauder Clark, and become part of Luton's Adult

Education Colleges Programme - Adtec - responsible for the College's Department of Religion. The church now provides evening classes in applied theology, and through the Luton Colleges can give recognised Diplomas.

Bramingham Park Centre (as the church is known) has a reputation for excellence in the field of education and theology in Luton.

- o O o -

Today, while the Study Centre operates upstairs, downstairs there is a hive of activities every day for Mums with babies, a creche, and a playgroup.

In fact the church is used every hour of the day for something, or as often as not - more than one.

All this 'downstairs' activity started out of the initial creche that I ran in the house, and the one that Pauline started for the Home tuition group.

What happened was that the two creches were amalgamated, and a daily Playgroup was begun. When we did a door to door survey asking people what they felt were the needs on the estate that the church could maybe help with, this was high up on the list of many shut-in Mums.

Because of local red-tape Pauline couldn't head up a registered playgroup herself, so Christine, one of the originals from Heather's Tuesday group, got a number of volunteers together to begin what was later called Jollytots. Unfortunately to Christine's amusement I kept calling it Jellytots.

Heather and I both wanted to be involved.

We loved playing with the children, helping them paint, make play-dough models, and to watch that they didn't fall off the indoor slide.

But legislation was getting tighter. All helpers had to be registered, and for this we all needed to fill in forms and then had to be 'checked out'.

It was great fun when some of us trotted off together to the local hospital to have blood samples taken and to be screened for this and that and they found a man walking in.

Not used to 'male helpers' for playgroups the hospital forms asked things about pregnancies etc. The nurse laughed as she looked at my midriff and wrote uncertainly 'No'.

On occasions Heather and I played our guitars for a sing-a-long time. We had to be careful of politically incorrect songs that the council disallowed. But what do you do when a child asks for it, and anyway does a sheep really feel prejudiced against because of its colour?

It was lovely that Christine asked all her helpers, whether they came to the church or not, to meet together for a prayertime before we began the day. This put everything on a spiritual footing.

One day a couple of Health Visitors who worked with the doctors opposite as well as with a number of other local surgeries, popped over into the church to talk about their desperate need to meet their new young mums in a Centre somewhere.

We already had a Mums and Toddlers group, called Sparklers, run by one of our church members, Michelle, and a committee she formed. This was a place where Mums could come with their 6mth to 4 year old children and let them play together while they shared their latest excitements - 'Peter has just cut his first tooth' - or latest woes - 'Zoe has developed this rash on her bum that won't go away', And there were Peter and Zoe sitting on the floor together happily slobbering on, and exchanging, the same plastic duck!!

I used to go and sing at this group to give the Mums a break while Michelle got the drinks ready.

We'd put the kiddy-chairs in a circle and I'd squat down on one to play. One fascinated Asian lad regularly toddled over and stuck his fingers between the strings of my guitar while we all sang together 'Ancient & Moderns' ranging from 'Here we go round the Mulberry Bush' to the latest TV jingles.

I still catch myself out singing 'The wheels on the bus go round and round.' - much to Heather's delight!!

So, we had groups for adults (Home Groups), a group for teenagers (Laser), groups for children (Rainbow Club), Jollytots for the 4 year olds down to 6 months, But there was nothing for first time Mums. So we felt excited when the Health Visitors suggested this Health Stop which would 'plug' the hole we had.

However, as a church. we felt that no matter how good the idea might be, like everything else in the church, it should be under our own supervision.

This posed no problems to Kate (the Health visitor) and her friend who both, we discovered in one of the more spiritual conversations that we often had, went to other churches.

Lesley, a young mum in our church with a small son, was asked if she would be willing to pray about supervising this new group for first time mums who were six months pregnant through until their babies were mobile (officially for Mums with babies from -6 months to +6 months). The group was appropriately called No.1.

So No 1, which included the Health Stop, started on Wednesdays in the church foyer/entrance, with Doris (one of our widowed pensioners) helping as registrar, tea maker, and washer-up-erer. The Health Visitors came each week and while the mums chatted and drank tea together they would check them out for any problems. On occasions they gave special talks on health matters.

At Christmas all these groups felt it was appropriate to have a short Carol Service. Logistically this was a headache. But a Carol Service gave a natural opportunity for Christians in the groups to share their faith more directly.

Often families would start coming to the church through one or more of these activities.

Our calling and commitment as a church to being a family meant not only being a church family, but being a family for everyone on Bramingham Park.

Chapter 11

Extension Work (continued)

The Rabbi on the radio, who I visualized as having a big smile and an expansive girth, said 'God taught our people through their senses, and especially through their stomachs.'

Food was something we enjoyed together right from the beginning of our story. In fact you can trace the history of Bramingham Park Church by the golden trail of crumbs that people left on route.

So maybe at this point Heather should take up the story - not that she was a crumb dropper, it's just that she is probably better equipped to guide you through this bit than me (and she makes the world's best crunchy dumplings).

- o O o -

'One can never guess the size of the final product from the embryonic idea.

One Wednesday, when the retired ladies' pilot group had finished a proof reading session on Zechariah and we had drunk yet more of Eva's coffee and prayed together, I decided that they deserved a little treat.

'Please come for lunch next Wednesday.'

Ruth, Millie, Marjorie and Eva (all widows on their own) came. We had such a riotous time that I invited them a month later. Month by month we ate together, and each time one or two extra ladies were invited to come too. It was like Topsy that 'just grew'd and grew'd'.

People were quick to offer help, and soon one of the greatest incentives for coming was to enjoy Majorie's apple pie!

Sue, Liz and Val Jeffers would often come early to help cook the vegetables and prepare the fruit salad - the slimmers alternative to Majorie's pies! Mary would come late, straight from work at the local chemists, and would help with the teas and coffees at the end of the meal.

By the time eighteen or twenty were eating lunch in our L-shaped room I started inviting a special guest each time as an after dinner speaker. Joyce, one of our neighbours, spoke about her work with victims of crime, and Janet, the curate of the local parish church, gave us a Lenten meditation from the Bible.

When we were about twenty five strong we spread our wings a little. People began making donations so that we could give a gift to the speakers who came. Thereby we were able to support the Salvation Army and various charities, and could invite people from farther afield like the London City Mission, and better known speakers.

We had decided that THIRTY was the limit for our kitchen (and front room) to cope with.

But by that stage we had the church building available, replete with large well-equipped kitchen. So rather than shrink the project we changed venue.

The next departure from the norm was to have lunches to which men as well as women were invited. Ryder could no longer bask in his male solitude.

As we met month by month there were many opportunities for those who knew Christ to share him with others in a very informal way. From time to time the after dinner speakers gave a specific Christian challenge, and some of the diners gave their lives to Christ or came back to a relationship with Jesus again.

Along with the Christian message I felt that these lunches had value as a means of friendship. Many regularly ate alone. Some had come to the estate from other areas and were feeling lonely. Some of those friendships made at the lunches are still going strong.

With hindsight I see the climax of the lunches as the time when we invited the regulars and all the past speakers to come again for a special guest speaker - Fiona Castle.

There were too many to eat comfortably in the entrance area of the church with its open bar kitchen. So the main worship area of the church was set out in a V-shape of tables.

Fiona spoke with passion and with humour about her life and her relationship with Jesus Christ.

That was a special occasion.

Very soon we were to take two further different turns.

The monthly Ladies Lunches changed. Instead of having this event once a month we began serving lunches every Tuesday not just for invited guests but for all who wanted to come. Elderly men and women, mothers with babies in prams, the unemployed, all were welcome.

We charged £1 for a meal (50p for children) and began to operate as a small restaurant (with necessary health inspection certificates) rather than a luncheon club.

Ryder (sporting bow tie and waistcoat) earned the nickname 'Manuel- from Barthelona' as he acted as head (and in the early days 'only') waiter.

Very soon extra help appeared. Christine and Margaret gave unstintingly of their time and energy in the kitchen - and Christine managed to keep Ryder in order (most of the time) with her quick wit.

People from other churches, such as Mary from the local Methodist church, and later Vin from the nearest Baptist church, became involved and expanded our view of 'the church'.

Peter was a great asset to us. Besides helping every week on Saturdays with the building he happily turned his fingers into prunes as he washed mountains of dirty dishes. He always kept going to the bitter end - all those greasy pans, messy ovens, teapots full of bags etc.! And he had plenty of muscle-power so he could lift and strain large containers of hot potatoes. He had a lively sense of humour, like Christine. When the two of them got going the rest of us ran for cover.

...he happily turned his fingers into prunes as he washed mountains of dirty dishes

You might be wondering what the customers ate for £1. How about a couple of sample menus.

****

MENU 1

Home made lasagna with chips
or jacket potato with various fillings and side salad
Bread and Butter
Rice pudding
or fruit salad
Tea or Coffee

****

MENU 2

Pork chop with potatoes, carrots and peas
or jacket potato with various fillings and side salad
Bread and butter
Jam Roly-poly with custard
or ice cream with a sauce
Tea or Coffee

****

We always gave a vegetarian alternative and provided children's portions.

As there were no wages to pay or overheads (apart from paying for our use of electricity to the church) with our profits we were able to buy for the church a freezer, all its crockery and cutlery, as well as keep the church stocked with such things as bin liners, washing up liquid, and cleaning materials - all from the customers' payments of £1.

With our 'easy access' ramps and disabled toilet we were able to cater for a wide range of people. Incidentally both the men's as well as women's toilets had baby changing facilities!

Directly opposite our front entrance across the road were the entrances to the health centre, chemist, post office and dentists, so as word got round we began catering for some of them too (not the dentist!). Mabel, from the surgery would make her order earlier in the day and fix a time to come over and eat, whereas often Ryder would be seen speeding across to the Post Office and Chemist in all weathers with trays of food.

The restaurant was something that we all consciously did

for the Lord. Because of that we were very happy working together and had lots of hilarious moments. Before we opened up for business and served food we stood round in a circle in our aprons and prayed together.

The rest of the time our faith sharing was more low-key, with leaflets available to explain the Christian message and many personal chats whilst taking orders. We had a room in the church we called the chapel which was always available for anyone who wanted to pray or be prayed for. On several occasions this was put to good use before or after someone's meal. One man even asked Ryder to pray with him between his main course and his sweet.

At Christmas we would serve a free meal - sometimes we needed three sittings to cope with the demand, and have a speaker who would talk for 5 or 10 minutes at each sitting. This way the Christian message of God's love in Christ would be shared with those who came.

One Christmas Peter Thompson from Biggleswade came to talk to about 80 festive people about the needs in Romania and a Romanian Aid Project that his church was involved in. We gave our gifts of money, but it went further than that, for God had touched our hearts. We had met Peter at one of the earlier ladies lunches when he told how his church was taking clothing into that needy country.

In co-operation with his project our own Romania Aid group started.

God had been challenging us about our comfortable lifestyle and the needs of the rest of the world, so when the Wednesday morning pilot group finished working through Haggai and Zechariah the ladies who came were ready for a change.

Each Wednesday we began to meet to sort, label and package new and good quality second-hand clothes that people in our church, or their friends, gave us.

We started praying for the people who would receive the goods and those who would transport them. When Peter came to collect the boxes of packed clothes and blankets that filled our garage he would tell us of specific needs and show photographs of Romanian people - which in turn fuelled our prayers and our enthusiasm'.

Frequently Peter asked the two of us to go with him to Eastern Europe. Each time we said 'No'. But through our involvement with Romania 'mission' gradually ascended the ladder of the church's interest and activity until some of us did go to Eastern Europe. Not Romania but Albania.

- o O o -

My Mum was a great plant enthusiast. On her kitchen window shelf behind the sink she had tied-up plastic bags with yoghurt pots inside containing planted orange and grapefruit pips.

'One day they will be trees.' she proudly stated as I looked sceptically for any sign of life.

Sure enough many years later I helped her in her Dorset garden to cover up for the winter a five foot grapefruit sapling.

I never forgot her words. Only a seed today, but later - a tree.

A vision of 'Christ's Family - in the community, for the Community' became a reality.

Our calling and commitment as a church to being a family meant not only being a church family, but being a family for everyone on Bramingham Park.

Being a family included being involved in as many aspects of family life on our estate as was practically possible.

Vision determines direction. Calling, character. Activities arise out of Aims.

However, it wasn't that we sat down one day and planned all the things we were going to do. Things sort of .... evolved, not willy nilly, but by sensing God's will for the next step. It was more like one step leading to the next.

Some churches have strategists (and there is nothing wrong in that) but we were more like God's ancient people.

After God freed them from being 'Builders of Bricks without Straw' they became 'Travellers without Maps'. All they had was a cloud to follow.

When I was a child my Dad would say on occasions 'Let's have a break somewhere'. 'Where are we going?' I would ask full of childish curiosity as we packed things into the car. 'Oh, I don't know. Let's go east this time and see where we end up.' he would smile. No sweat for me. He was in charge.

God's people didn't take any old road to see where it ended up. But imagine the embarrassment of being asked by a curious son, 'Dad, what are we doing? Where are we going?' and having to say, 'Well son, we're following that cloud.'

Weird.

But the thing was, God was in the cloud.

We were a bit like that. A pilgrim people following the cloud. Where it went we went. Where it stayed we stayed. Or we were trying to.

For us it was not just a matter of 'bricks without straw', but 'pilgrims without maps'.

Unnerving, but exciting.

The trick was to keep one eye constantly on the cloud to see where it was moving, and then to run with it.

So, out of Heather's Tuesday Pilot Group came a creche that ended up with creches, playgroups, Mums and kids groups (now, 'Parents and Offspring' as some Dads go), and a Health Stop.

Into our concern and care for the marginalised came Jan's vision for Home Tuition, and out of that the Bramingham Park Study Centre and Adult Education.

Out of a Wednesday lunch came Lunches with speakers, the Restaurant, hearing about and helping Europe; through the Romanian project came a concern for mission and eventually the sending of the church's first two missionaries.

Chapter 12

An Inspector calls

The big question in our minds was 'Will it be okay? Will it pass the test? Would we get our certificate?' Although we were in our property and life was running on at a pace this was the day that the Building Inspector was coming to give us what we hoped would be the final inspection that would declare the whole property 'fit for human habitation' or something like that. We had survived the inspections of footings and foundations, drains and plumbing, electricity and gas installations, but this was the inspection of the finished structure.

Unfortunately it wasn't David the architect's friend but another person.

When he arrived he started to look here and there, up and down, in and out, and made notes.

Eventually he faced me and said, 'I'm not happy with one of the velux window joints where it meets the roof truss, there need to be a few more noggins to stop the upstairs floor joists from warping. and I have found some putlog holes not filled'. I thought of the pudlog holes where the scaffolding was secured into the walls during building in MY house. There were loads of them not filled by the professionals - but I bit my tongue.

'Thanks.' I said, 'We'll tell you when they are finished.'.

A month later he returned to look us over again. I held my breath as he looked (almost with a magnifying glass) at the parts he had questioned before as though longing to find something wrong.

Eventually he found something - one putlog hole not filled. With a visible straightening of his shoulders he turned and pronounced, 'I have found a hole not filled. You will receive your certificate - but you must fill in that hole.'

The big question in church life is, 'Will it stand the test - the test of time and the storms of life?', 'How will the structures fare?'

In one sense, as far as church is concerned. the work is never finished until what we call The Last Day, when the Architect, Supervisor and Inspector of the whole universe, comes.

People who think that anything spiritual is finished before then are living in a dream world.

People had come to faith in Jesus - but that wasn't the end.

People had started meeting together for worship - but that wasn't it.

There were those who had wanted to be baptised as a witness to their faith. How do you do that in a Sales Information Office? Well, we managed to get hold of an 8x4foot structure with 4x4inch timbers that held together pieces of plywood with 10inch carriage bolts. This box then had a swimming pool lining put inside which we we filled with water from a hose and emptied with buckets! But baptism wasn't the end.

Gifting teams had developed and church leadership had emerged, but that wasn't the end.

We had gone from home to A-frame, and then into our own property. We had built, had entered, and finished stage one of it, and had packed it out with all those who had been involved in any stage of its development to celebrate at the Official Opening. But that wasn't the end.

It's interesting to read in our final prayer letter before leaving Bramingham how we wrote ' We have decided as a church to extend the property another three metres to provide a much needed store downstairs and a staircase to open up upstairs.'

And then we as a couple were to leave, called by God to work elsewhere (more about that later), but that wasn't the end.

The Place and People

Things weren't to be allowed to grind to a halt because we were going - after all, the work wasn't to depend on us. That's how we had planned it. Faith still needed to be stretched and strengthened - theirs and ours.

So, how's it all gone? What happened to the church? How did it stand up to the test of us leaving and going off to Albania and the test of time?

It was certainly testing to the faith of those in leadership!

Again in that last letter Heather and I asked our prayer supporters, 'Please pray for Bramingham at this difficult time of change, especially for the leaders. Many have never been in leadership before, most have never gone through the process of saying goodbye to their old minister and wife. Pray that the whole church will hold together in the love of Jesus, grow in faith (this year's motto is 'Lord, I believe, help my unbelief'), and be protected from the attacks of the devil through well and ill-intended people.'

As soon as the Lord had showed us and the church about the extension of the church's mission abroad, we spent a great deal of time trying to prepare the leaders for how it would be without us, and got them to share their vision and fears for the future without us.

How did people react to the leaving of what to many seemed the 'Mum and Dad' of the family?

Reactions ranged from shock, sadness, pessimism, to a sense of rightness, excitement and optimism about the future.

Basically there were two types of reaction to us going in the leadership and the church. Those who sensed that this was a new stage for growth and that the Lord was going to do some new things for us in Albania and for them at Bramingham. Generally they were enthusiastic about the possibilities.

Then there were those who were thrown into uncertainty - a bit like the first time the stabilisers are taken off a child's bike, or a person in a glider without his instructor.

We had tried over the years to release people into their gifting, and hand responsibility over to others, but naturally we still tended to be thought of as the hub of things - with Jesus, of course, as the spindle for it all. Over the years we had tried to get the teams to take over our jobs and the leaders to take over our place.

Naturally there were those in the church who had got emotionally tied to us - but then genuine love does create bonds. The problem is when bonds become shackles because shackles stop people from moving on.

When later we returned from Albania for a break, well-meaning people would say, 'It's not been the same since you left'. To which we replied 'Should it be?' The classic came when the minister the church called after us, left to work in Ireland. One dear person said to us, 'Now you can have your old job back. You can even have your old house back' Gently we pointed out that it is wrong to try to turn the clock back. We need to look to the new things that the Lord has in mind for our future.

One of the questions about the future that the leaders and church had to face was, should they continue without an outside leader/minister, or should they actively look for someone?

On the one side some leaders said that after we left and they had to go it alone, they grew up as leaders. The further time went on the stronger they became. One put it like this, 'Pain develops people'. Whether that was physical pain, moral pain, emotional pain or spiritual pain (and they faced all of these) no one could remain the same.

On the other hand some felt with the passing of time, despite personal growth, a weakening of the structures and relationships.

It's interesting to hear some of the reasons given for the decision to choose and call a full-time minister.

'We needed a co-ordinator', 'We needed a new vision'. 'We needed help'. A foreboding of divisiveness, because certain individuals wanted to take more on themselves than they should, made others feel the need for an outside arbitrator.

Constantly we had stressed to the leaders before we left, that Biblical leadership is all about service. Jesus was clearly against power politics. There were the times he told off the first leaders in his church (the apostles) when they sought to get the best seats in the kingdom, and wanted to get a pecking order of who was the greatest. Jesus said that the greatest was the least and the servant of all.

On the other hand, it seems that a few people mixed up in

the 'Servanthood' issue the ideas of not wanting to push themselves forward, and indecisiveness - one being true and the other not. At times I sensed from a distance that it unfortunately happened the other way round.

Leaders, we had said, need to remember that they are to be ongoing learners, shepherds, and models by their humble service and love.

We warned that a leader is part of a team, not only of the teams that they had been called to work in, but also with one another. Was that the reason Jesus sent his disciples out two by two?.

If, however, you have a team leader who is not a team player you've got problems. Sadly throughout the church of Jesus Christ many leaders (whether they are in youth work, church departments, elders, deacons or even ministers) today aren't team players. They want to lead, but can't be led, they want others to give account but don't want to be accountable.

Was that one of the reason the leadership team was reduced?

I don't know that everyone completely understood that message, or that it was heard. Initially things went well but with the passing of time it seems that 'people power' created a bit of a pull in different directions.

Some felt with the passing of time that the leadership team was too large, at times divided between those who saw things practically and those spiritually, those who wanted to press forward and those hold back.

A sense of obligation to the denomination and its expectations about a minister was expressed. Pressure from society with the changing of laws, for example the Children's Act that called for greater accountability, was also felt and caused 'a bit of a flap'.

Because the leaders saw the potential of pulling in two directions they looked for a minister who would primarily seek God's will, be flexible, still challenge the traditions, teach God's Word and disciple the family, and unite the people for new challenges.

So what about the teams?

Because of the principle established in the church, to avoid inflexibility (traditions, and some workers, soon get set in concrete!), that all gifts and ministries were to be reviewed annually, some of the leaders thought that not only were their ministries to be temporary, but maybe also the whole concept of gifting.

We had tried to create an 'open ended' church family where people with dramatic encounters and experiences of the Holy Spirit and those without could live and serve together.

Of course there were always the tensions of those who understood and used 'spiritual gifts' wanting to race ahead, and those who didn't not wanting to be exposed to them. But a bit of tension never harmed anyone. In fact doctors explain that without any muscular tension our bodies couldn't function!

Anyway, Paul in his letter to the first Christian church in Rome says, 'The gifts and calling of God are without recall.'

How they operate can be.

After our leaving, a number of years later, the concept of teams was questioned and some teams stopped functioning.

A few of the reasons seem to have been practical, some spiritual.

For example, people moving away from the area made the structures too stretched. There were major family crises for some families that caused obstacles. The integrity and obedience of others became a significant hurdle. A changing vision about the method and use of gifting and teams made a difference. And of course the usual dampener that affects so many churches, the pressure of work, smothered a great deal!!

Despite all this, gifts are still operating, though in a different way. Sometimes in the more traditional way of through just one person in the church - which does seem to be a natural gravitational action if it is not held back. Some teams are operating combined under one person.

At this present moment after a new touch of God, gifts seem to be re-emerging.

Some of the the teams, though organised differently, are still functioning in a changed form.

Due to the reduction or non-functioning of various teams, due to a new system of pastoral care based in home groups, due to a loss of energy and a period of change, the form of leadership in the church has changed, but is still based on the principle of gifting.

I like the comment of one person who has remained in the church until now, 'You were the catalysts for the vision. Though things went through a period of change after you left, with a different style of leadership, and the teams concept being different, the principles so firmly rooted have stayed. People know that we are to be a family and the church is still encouraging gifting in people.'

That sounds like something Heather wrote earlier.

- o O o -

'We returned from Albania to England for the blessing/dedication of our grandson Aaron.

The next day was the funeral of Simon - aged 32 - a key person in the work and growth of the church, spanning the end of our time into the first years of ministry of Lauder Clark, our successor.

A bitter, sweet weekend.

Two things struck me. The vision continues, the people move on.

The vision of 'A Family' is still there. Both services, by the way the room was arranged, by the participation of many, and by the presence of all ages (even at the funeral) demonstrated that we are still His Family.

The expansion and extension into the community has surpassed our wildest dreams, New ventures of faith are continually being followed (and that's yet another story).

Of the people who worshipped with us in our house at the start of everything only Roy, Paul and Rachel remained.

The original people have scattered to New Zealand, Canada, Jamaica, Wales, and Albania, many are in heaven, some have lost the vision they had, but ...... His work goes on.....'

It goes on in Albania, as well as Luton, through others catching the vision.

Chapter 13

Topping Off

So what about us two church planters?

As we stretched out on the beach in California I crooned to Heather the old 50's song of Pat Boone 'When the swallows come back to Capistrano.'

This was the life, sunbathing and swimming at S.Juan Capistrano Beach on the advice and encouragement of Bob Fulton, one of the Pastors of the Anaheim Vineyard!

We were on part of a Sabbatical - which means 'rest'.

When God had finished his work of creation he had a well earned rest and called that rest 'the Sabbath', and now after seven years hard work we also needed a bit of a break.

We hadn't finished our work, but we had done a great deal. We had seen a spiritual church family built from nothing to a church operating with recognised and gifted leadership and functioning as a light of justice and love for the society in which it was placed. We'd seen a physical church building constructed from ground level (or below!!) through its various stages up to the roof being topped off by John Deveney ceremoniously banging down the last stack-pipe cover.

But there was to be more. We felt that something was missing.

Then the answer came - we needed not only to be a light of justice and love to our own community where we lived, we needed to reach the world. We needed a world vision.

In fact before we went off for our break, at one service as we were waiting on God to hear what he wanted to say, Heather passed over to me as the leader of that particular service a note. On it she had written: 'I believe that God is saying that there are two people here that he wants to serve him overseas'. So I read it out, and waited.

None so blind as those who cannot see. We were looking to others and not to ourselves.

Anyway, we were now having a well earned rest in the big U.S of A.

'Why have you come here?' Bob asked us.

'To meet the Lord afresh and to hear from him.' we replied.

Sensing in his spirit that he was talking to a somewhat overworked and overtired couple (we had just gone through a most exhausting year with the marriages of our two daughters and the death of my mother, all the demands of busy church life as well as the official opening of the church building) and seeing two people who had a deep longing for spiritual refreshment, but needed a good rest, he unexpectedly though wisely said, 'The Lord can meet you on the beach, not just in church, you know.'

So we enjoyed fourteen of California's best beaches - including Bay Watch Beach, which was disappointingly deserted. Who said that? Ryder or Heather?

Avoiding places like Disney Land, Hollywood and Notts Farm (a smaller version of Disney land - not a real farm), and escaping as quickly as possible the spiritual oppression of Las Vegas (an unavoidable stop-over), we went to awe inspiring places like Bryce National Park, Zion National Park, Grand Canyon, Death Valley, and Yosemite National Park (besides others) where we felt the majesty and power of our God.

But it was in Lancaster, California, that the Lord especially came and spoke to us.

We had gone there to check out a prophecy given to me in front of 400 leaders at a Chorleywood Clergy Conference by the pastor of the Lancaster Vineyard, Brent Rue, some ten months before.

'Because of the way you that view the Kingdom, life and ministry, the Lord says 'I'm moving you into places that you would be frightened in your own ability to do. It's way over my head, well, I couldn't do this'. Let me just say this, If the Lord brings opportunities, know that he doesn't want to change you. It is because he has fashioned and formed you for the ministry to conform around you. The strength you have is who you are in Christ, and he can take you in many doors because of that one.'

That had impacted me like a bolt out of the blue - God is a bit like that.

At the time I was questioning my ministry and methodology - what with all the debate in our church about family worship and the children. 'Know that he doesn't want to change you. It is because he has fashioned and formed you for the ministry to conform around you. The strength you have is who you are in Christ.' What an encouragement and help that was in solving my immediate question.

But through that word the Lord gently opened another door in my mind. 'The Lord says 'I'm moving you into places that you would be frightened in your own ability to do. It's way over my head, well, I couldn't do this. Let me just say this, If the Lord brings opportunities, know that he doesn't want to change you.....'

We had always practised a principle in our ministry. If the Lord called us to a place, we were there to stay, if necessary for the rest of our lives. That stopped us from getting itchy feet.

I always remember a telephone call after we had been in our first church for just three years - the minimum time required to fulfil the probationary period. 'You've been in Tiverton three years now? I expect you'll be looking for a change,' said a church secretary from somewhere in London. Surprised by his assumption I, without thinking, said simply 'No.' 'Oh,' he replied 'Oh, well God bless you in what you are doing.' and the line went dead.

Despite this principle of 'there to stay' we were always ready to pray, and be available for the Lord to move us on and out. So what was this about 'I'm moving you into places that you would be frightened in your own ability to do?'

As we were walking round the local park in the centre of Lancaster, by Brent's church, that October in 1992, it came.

'I want you to go to Albania..........after Easter.'

'Why?' we wanted to know.

There was silence.

'Oh, Oh, that's familiar.' we thought, as we reflected on the beginnings of our church planting experiences.

'Maybe the Lord is testing us like Abraham. Maybe he just wants to see if we love him' we thought to ourselves.

He was testing our love. He was also testing our obedience.

After Easter we flew to Corfu, spent a night sitting on our cases by the quayside of the wrong port, managed to catch the

6.00am local bus to the right one, lost my purse with all my money in it, ran back through Corfu Town to the bus depot and managed to retrieve it, ended up with migraine (the second in my whole life) but eventually caught the ferry and arrived in the southern Albanian port of Saranda.

...a night sitting on our cases by the quayside of the wrong port

Having learned earlier a few words and phrases of that most difficult of languages that we are still trying to fully understand after five years (Yes, Brent was right, certainly 'Frightening in our own ability to do. Way over our head', and at our age!), we wandered along the sun-drenched but crumbling promenade, practising our 'Tungjatjeta'-s (hello) as we waited to be met by two BMS missionaries. Chris Burnett and Steve Alford who were coming in a van with Zef their driver to take us on a six and a half hour journey back through Albania to Tirana the capital.

Albania had become a democracy less than three years before our visit. For 50 years she had endured the most exclusivistic communist atheistic dictatorship in the world.

After two wonderful weeks in that beautiful, hospitable, but broken down country, we returned, via Saranda again, to the culture shock of mixing with pot bellied British beer-swigging, chip-eating, constantly-complaining holiday makers on Corfu.

Standing at the stern of our little ferry, as Albania receded into the distance, tears welled up in my eyes for that needy land.

Then the whisper came. 'Now you have my heart, you can return .... full time.'

So we called together our leadership team and asked them to test our call.

Ironically, at the beginning of that year I had said that I felt that our church needed a greater missionary involvement and should pray about our church sending out missionaries. Little did we realise or reckon on the fact that we would be the answer to that thought!

When the leadership team, and all the church, confirmed this to be the Lord's call and that we should become the church's first missionaries, we gave in our notice and applied to the Baptist Missionary Society.

Within six months were walking the muddy streets of the capital - Tirana - saying to one another as we walked hand in hand under the starlight sky. 'This is our new home. This is where we are to build more churches.'

There was certainly enough mud to make lots of bricks - and straw in plenty (laden on the backs of poor little donkeys which made them look like walking haystacks with protruding ears) to bind them together!

- oOo -

Within six months of our arrival after a crash course in Albanian we found ourselves in a 'village' (of 10,000 people!!) called Bregu-i-Lumit, or in English 'Riverside'. This however was not quite as attractive as it sounds.

Once, when asked by an Albanian from the capital where we lived he reacted to our reply with surprise, a turned down lip and a comment of disdain.

We discovered later that during the communist era a great number of political and social rejects had been placed in our village and that it was considered the lowest of the low.

Despite both Albanian and missionary comments about 'I would never live there' we believed that 'mission' begins with 'incarnation'. In other words, you don't sit outside the situation and theorise, you actually get into it, live in it, and work it out with the people you are trying to touch.

Jesus did that when he left the peace and beauty of heaven and came to live on earth. Not only that but he chose a working class family in a village of socially deprived 'rejects' and political hot-heads - 'Can anything good come out of Nazareth?' people said in his day.

So he came and he stayed there despite all the darkness. He didn't pop back to heaven for a good night's sleep and re-evaluation. He lived the message, day in, day out. That's what we had to do. And we do it because we love the Lord and love the people of our village.

We are simply trying to live out what we believe.

Even with a dog!

Dogs in Albania are only good for two things - throwing stones at or as 'wild' guards.

After being burgled twice in our first month and having seven other attempted break-ins, we decided to get a dog.

When Roj (pronounced Roy and meaning in Albanian 'Guard') arrived as a little puppy we were immediately advised to shut him up in a dark shed all day without food then at night give him something to eat when we let him out. He would then be wild and bite everything apart from the hand that fed him.

But that would be no use when starting a church in our home and the dog got out and bit everyone - apart from getting us quickly into prayer for healing from all the dog bites!!

So, to the amusement and amazement of the neighbours, we started to train the dog to sit, wait, come, and bark on command.

Eyes popped out in disbelief as I took the dog for a WALK on a lead!! 'These English are crazy.' they thought, but more politely asked, 'What are you doing?'

'Walking the dog.' I explained 'Training him to be a good guard dog.'

'Why not shut him up in a shed all day?'

This was now the opportunity to explain the Christian message. How? I hear you say.

'When God created the world he said that humans had the responsibility to care for his creation - creatures as well as crops. We're just obeying God.'

Well, that's a new way to start sharing the Christian message!

Interestingly a week or two later I saw a child dragging behind him a puppy on a piece of string.

'What you doing?' I asked.

'Doing the same as you with Roj.' came the reply.

He was learning.

In starting a new work, especially in a new culture, one must always start anew.

The biggest danger is to say that because something worked in one place it will necessarily work in another. We had to understand the people, the language and the culture.

How awful to import our way of thinking and doing things. How disastrous to import the limitations of our culture when we are called to give the liberation of God's Kingdom.

However we did begin in Albania as we began in Luton. We did say to the Lord once again 'It's your church, build it your way.'

Many of the basics that we had thrashed out in the UK after prayer we felt at ease to apply in Albania.

They were:
>First: to open up the Bible - God's Word.
>Second: to point people to Jesus as Lord.
>Third: to follow only Him.

It's interesting to see that we have a number of banners in our church in Bregu-i-Lumit that people have made that focus on these three points.

Three specifically say, in Albanian of course, 'Your Word is a lamp that shines on my road' (Psalm 119:103), 'Jesus is Lord' (Philippians 2:11), and 'Come after Me' (Mark 1:16).

We demonstrated these three principles in practice as we talked naturally to our neighbours when they asked 'Where are you from? Why have you come here from England - it's the place we want to go to?'

'God told us to come here', we told them, and off we went into the story of our first visit after the Lord said 'Go to Albania.'

It amazed people that God should actually speak to us.

After 50 years of atheistic teaching that there is no God, and earlier Muslim teaching that God is great and high in heaven, this was a revelation!

That then opened the door to talking about his love for creation (especially Albania which many Albanians regard as under the curse of God). This led naturally to tell how Jesus came to earth to call people to follow him. The Bible would be quoted here and there, and an invitation given to come along to our house to hear more.

As people have opened their hearts to Jesus, read the Bible, nailed their colours to the mast in baptism in the sea, the Lord has released his gifts (often without our doing anything). Visions and prophecies have become the norm. Prayer became a high priority, (in fact many folk's first visit to our work was to the prayer time) and answers have come to these prayers with a healing here and a healing there.

God has given real hearts and gifts of worship. A worship group was started from scratch, and now the 5 guitars, bass guitar, violin, keyboard and drums are led by a young Albanian girl of 19. Many original songs, obviously in Albanian, have been written and are regularly sung by the church family.

Young people have learned to share what God has shown them without fear or embarrassment, and so teaching gifts have started to appear and mature. We have been able to call on at least seven young people to speak at the Sunday services. Our youngest 'preacher' was a 12 year old boy whose message would have shaken many English congregations for its insight and power.

Risky? Yes. But as Martyn Joseph the Welsh song writer says in his song 'Do it', 'Faith is spelt R-I-S-K.'

We have a practical team who serve refreshments half way through the Sunday service, and a couple of 'body-builders' who act more like bouncers at an English nightclub than church stewards, who guard the door and gently 'remove' any problem people.

One of the young people has developed a heart for telling his neighbours about Jesus and has organised a door to door visitation programme. Twice a week up to four teams go out on the doors to tell people about the good news of Jesus.

So some things have developed similarly, others very differently, but the Lord is always original - Thank God.

That's why we tell the church that it needs to keep its eyes not on us and our ideas but on Jesus and his ways.

We have been privileged to bring three of our young people back to our sending church in Luton (two in 1996, and one in 1998) where they have been able to tell what God has done for them and through them.

The blessing we took from Luton to Albania, as well as the lessons that we learned, have turned round full circle as Christians from Bregu-i-Lumit have come to Bramingham Park and blessed them.

So the work of God increases, going from here to there and back again, and who knows where.... until all the bricks are made, churches built, and the one world-wide Church of Jesus Christ completed.

But, in all this, we need to constantly keep in mind something that is sung in one of the songs the Lord has given to our church in Albania:

Si ta ndërtojmë kishen tënde Jezusi?	How can we build your church, Jesus?
Si ta ndërtojmë kishen tënde këtu?	How can we build your church here?
Si ta ndërtojmë kishen tënde Jezusi?	How can we build your church, Jesus?
Nuk është e mundur -	It's not possible -
Fare, fare, fare.	Never, never, never.
Vetëm Ti ke mundësi,	Only You have the ability,
Vetëm Ti ke mundësi,	Only You have the ability,
Vetëm Ti ke mundësi.	Only You have the ability.
Zot, ndërto,	Lord, build,
Zot, mbretëro,	Lord, reign,
Zot, ndërto	Lord, build
Kishen tënde.	Your church.

© Elena e Flutura

Chapter 14

Epilogue

Jesus promised:
'I will build MY church',
even if at times it seems to us to be built of bricks without straw.

APPENDICES

1.	Values of the Church	144
2.	Church Commitment. Covenant, Confession & Constitution	145
3.	Work Sharing and Faith Sharing Questionnaire	151
4.	Team Profiles	154
5.	Leadership Models	163
6.	Countdown History of our Church	167
7.	Leaflet about Jehovah's Witnesses	170
8.	Attendance Graph	171
9.	Apostolic Persons and People	172
	Study Guide	176

Appendix 1

VALUES of the Church

'Values' are about the things that are important to us. They are focal points that help people know how a group operates, and factors that help it to decide what to do.

So we evolved and produced the following five points -

The VALUES that help us to decide issues are:

1. THE LORDSHIP OF JESUS CHRIST

    The Church is His (He died for it, and now lives in it - His People).

    He is in charge, so His will is preeminent.

2. THE BIBLE

    We accept the reliability and authority of the Bible, and seek to check out everything by this.

3. THE HOLY SPIRIT

    We believe that He is active, as in the Bible, in power to help, speak and heal today.

4. THE INDIVIDUAL

    Each person is of value to the Lord, and to us, no matter what their age, circumstances, race or sex. All can hear from God. Knowing and doing what He says to us personally is of primary importance. Individuality must be respected and love be unconditional.

5. PEOPLE MATTER MORE THAN THINGS

    Our priorities are:

    i) sharing the good news that Christ died, is risen and will come again.

    ii) personal growth. Property and programmes are secondary.

Appendix 2

CHURCH COMMITMENT, COVENANT, CONFESSION and CONSTITUTION

Things in our church life developed slowly, or evolved in stages.

We began with something very basic and practical ie. with a simple statement of Commitment. That later became a part of a Covenant we made with the Lord and one another. That covenant was to identify ourselves as a people of God (a church) living together in a relationship that was deeper than just out of personal preference.

These two were finally encapsulated in a Constitution together with a very simple and basic Confession

One of the hardest things for established churches to do is to separate Principles from Practices, but it is vital because Practices change, Principles continue.

When writing Constitutions people try to safeguard things by putting in lots of practices that may be appropriate at the time, but later have problems when it comes to changing them. Someone at a church meeting is sure to object on the basis of the Constitution. In fact in one church after explaining something that the Bible clearly said a leader stood up and said 'It doesn't matter what the Bible says, our constitution says.'. Something is desperately wrong when that happens!

So at the beginning of this new work we decided to follow the KISS method - 'Keep It Simple, Son'

Our first Constitution had to be tidied up and slightly amended for legal purposes.

So here are the stages we went through.

Commitment.

Stage 1 in the early days was a simple 3fold commitment of love.

'Our Commitment is to Love
> the Lord,
> one another,
> those needing Jesus.'

Stage 2 was extended into some practical applications (after all we can understand love in different ways). To this we added some Bible verses to show what we were basing our commitment on.

'Our Commitment is to Love
- the Lord and obey his word
    Mark 12v30; John 14v15
- one another as we are unconditionally
    John 13v34-35; 15v13
- those needing Jesus to bring them to know him
    Matthew 28v19-20'

Stage 3 was to extend this Commitment into a Covenant that people signed as an outward sign of who was actually committed to the Lord, one another and the work we were doing. This annual covenant showed who really were identified with us, and it was signed annually to provide a 'dynamic membership' role. People who no longer attended or who didn't sign were no longer members. We didn't have to discipline or remove members; by default non-participating/non-attending people lapsed their membership.

The Covenant Roll was available on a side table at every communion service as we celebrated the Lord's Covenant sealed with his blood. People, as they remembered, renewed or entered into a personal covenant with the Lord, were able to sign up. Despite this monthly availability we had a complete renewal of covenant for everyone every September (our birthday).

Covenant.

We COVENANT ourselves as the Family of God on Bramingham Park, Luton,
   to the Lord Jesus and to one another to:
   worship and serve the Lord,
   teach and obey his Word,
   love and serve one another,
   make and baptise disciples,
   and bear witness in the power of the Holy Spirit to
       Christ crucified, risen, and coming again.

When we finalised our Constitution we included a simple confession as follows:

Confession.

'We individually CONFESS Jesus Christ as 'My Lord and my God', accept the authority of the Bible, and

seek to live under the Lordship of Jesus Christ in the power of the Holy Spirit.

Stage 4. **Constitution.**

Much discussion within a church, and much pressure from outside, often goes into a constitution as it is the legal basis for a society, group, or organisation.

People can get diverted into minutiae (ie Rules and Regulations), that eventually become restricting rather than liberating.

Consequently we evolved a Constitution that was as simple as possible to explain who we were and what we did.

'Principles', that we felt we would not want to change, needed stating clearly, but 'Practices', which alter according to circumstances and what the Lord may be saying at any specific time, needed to be kept to a minimum retaining only basic practices.

First Constitution

'BRAMINGHAM PARK CHURCH is made up of people who have made a COMMITMENT to

'Love the Lord and obey His Word (Mk12:30;Jn14:15)
one another as we are unconditionally (Jn 13:34,35; Jn 15:13)
and those needing Jesus, to bring them to know Him (Matt 28:19,20)

who wish to COVENANT themselves 'As the Family of God on Bramingham Park, Luton, to the Lord Jesus and to one another to worship and serve the Lord; teach and obey His Word; love and serve one another; make and baptise disciples; and bear witness in the power of the Holy Spirit to Christ crucified, risen and coming again'

Each covenanted person CONFESSES

'Jesus Christ as "My Lord and my God";

accepts the authority of the Bible; and seeks to live under the Lordship of Jesus Christ in the power of the Holy Spirit.

Those who are covenanted together will seek to meet regularly, in the context of worship, to discover the mind of God. Due notice of such gatherings, and of any special occasions, shall be given to enable personal preparatory prayer.

A record of such discoveries and decisions shall be kept.

Everyone committed to Jesus Christ is important within the Family. All are to encouraged to discover and exercise the gifts and ministries the Lord may give in the power of the Spirit.

Together the covenanted people will recognise and set aside those who demonstrate and exercise the spiritual gifts of leadership and administration, the majority of these should have been baptised as believers.

The overseeing minister should be one who demonstrates the gifts and graces necessary for this role, who is able and willing to participate in the Commitment, Covenant, and Confession of the Church, has been baptised as a believer, and is received by the covenanting people as one called by the Holy Spirit to minister with them as part of God's family on Bramingham Park.'

After a period of prayer and discussion within the church three extra paragraphs were added: 'These gatherings may be called by either the leadership or by a minimum on 10 of the covenanted family - due public notice being given.

Bramingham Park Church seeks to be in fellowship with all the Family of God and holds an open membership policy whilst being a part of the Bedfordshire Baptist Association and affiliated to the Baptist Union of Great Britain

All gifts and ministries should be prayerfully evaluated personally by each individual as well as by the leadership and covenanted members after the annual covenant service.'

After correspondence with the 'powers that be' outside the church the whole thing was then 'tidied up' re-adjusted and put into an orderly fashion to include the principles of foundations, membership, service, and minimal practices.

Final Constitution

'BRAMINGHAM PARK CHURCH (a part of the Bedfordshire Baptist Association and affiliated to the Baptist Union of Great Britain) seeks to be in fellowship with all the Family of God and so holds an open membership policy.

1. Membership. The Church Family is made up of people who

i) have made a COMMITMENT

to 'Love the Lord and obey His Word (Mk12:30;Jn14:15)
one another as we are unconditionally (Jn 13:34,35; Jn 15:13)
those needing Jesus, to bring them to know Him (Matt 28:19,20)

ii) wish to COVENANT themselves 'As the Family of God on Bramingham Park, Luton, to the Lord Jesus and to one another to worship and serve the Lord; teach and obey His Word; love and serve one another; make and baptise disciples; and bear witness in the power of the Holy Spirit to Christ crucified, risen and coming again'

iii) individually CONFESS 'Jesus Christ as "My Lord and my God"; accept the authority of the Bible; and seek to live under the Lordship of Jesus Christ in the power of the Holy Spirit.

2. Meetings. Usually on Sundays the Church Family will join together for worship and prayer; fellowship and ministry; to hear and share God's Word; celebrate communion at least once a month; to administer believers' baptism as required.

Those who are covenanted together will seek to meet regularly, in the context of worship, to discover the mind of God at least once a quarter. Due notice of such gatherings, and of any special occasions, shall be given to enable personal preparatory prayer. A record of such discoveries and decisions shall be kept.

These gatherings may be called for either by the leadership or by a minimum of 10 of the covenanted family - due notice being given.

A special meeting shall be called to appoint or to dismiss the overseeing Minister, to deal with the sale or purchase of Church property, or to alter the Constitution of the Church. At least two weeks written notice must be given to each member; and, as long as not less than one half of the members shall be present, such a resolution shall be passed by a majority of two thirds of the members present voting.

3. Ministry. i) Everyone committed to Jesus Christ is important within the Family. All are encouraged to discover and exercise the gifts and ministries the Lord may give in the power of the Holy Spirit.

Together the covenanted people will recognise and set aside

those who demonstrate and exercise the spiritual gifts of leadership and administration out of each ministry. The majority of these should have been baptised as believers.

All gifts and ministries should be prayerfully evaluated personally by each individual as well as by the leadership and covenanted members after the annual covenant service.

ii) the overseeing minister should be one who demonstrates the gifts and graces necessary for this role; who is able and willing to participate in the Commitment, Covenant, and Confession of the Church; has been baptised as a believer; who should appear on the accredited lists of the Baptist Union of Great Britain; and is received by the covenanting people as one called by the Holy Spirit to minister with them as part of God's family on Bramingham Park'

Appendix 3

WORK SHARING AND FAITH SHARING

After people had come to faith in Jesus the next stage was to release them into service and ministry.

We did this by teaching about gifts and abilities that the Lord gives to his disciples and gave out the following explanation form and questionnaire.

Information attached to questionnaire:

WORK-SHARING AND FAITH SHARING IN OUR CHURCH

Nobody is being told 'If you come to this church you must do one of these jobs'

You may be over-stretched already and have many demands on your time and energy. You may not be well and strong enough to tackle anything else. Maybe you don't want to be involved at the moment.

This list is to show what the needs are, so that those who do want to be involved, and are free to be, can see what the options are.

You may see many possibilities for yourself on the list. Perhaps it would be best to aim for one main area of involvement with possibly one or two subsidiary ones. It would be a mistake to attempt too much.

What we are is more important than what we do. We are all equally valued and important to God, and He loves each of us infinitely. Our gifts, abilities, and opportunities differ.

The main question is:

What does the Lord Jesus want me to do?

SAMPLE QUESTIONNAIRE

to initiate and release ministry in the church

WORK-SHARING & FAITH-SHARING in our CHURCH FAMILY

The main question is:

WHAT DOES THE LORD JESUS WANT ME TO DO? See Acts 22 v 10.

How is God leading? Please tick your area of interest or ability.

WORSHIP/MUSIC Team involves practice and teaching alternate Wednesday evenings, and prayer/preparation before Sunday Worship. For singers, musicians, composers. Please state which instrument(s) .... ☐

PASTORAL Team visits/telephones/sends cards/flowers etc. in the event of sickness/new home/bereavement/new baby/personal crisis etc., welcomes people, cares and listens. Team meets about every six weeks to share, plan and pray. ☐

PRAYER MINISTRY Team prays for and with those who request prayer (both 'one-off' and 'on-going') for spiritual/physical/emotional healing.

The team meets fortnightly for training and prayer. ☐

SECRETARIAL Team includes typing, taking notes/minutes, keeping records, printing, producing rotas, directories, magazines, dealing with correspondence, using photocopier and computer. Team meets quarterly for planning and prayer. ☐

FINANCE Team counts offerings, banks money, keeps accounts, deals with covenants, gifts, payments, and the church budget. The team meets regularly (at least once a quarter) for prayer, planning and teaching. ☐

TEACHING Team plans the overall teaching programme for the church family, and is involved in teaching in small and large groups for men, women, and children, and in training others to teach. Team meets regularly for prayer, teaching and planning. ☐

PRAYER CORE Team is responsible for prayer chain, days of prayer, prayer triplets, keeping prayer at the centre of church life in many, varied ways. Meets as a group together when appropriate. ☐

ARTS Team includes banner making, flower arranging, sketches, dance, poetry, dramatic Bible reading, table decorations, embroidery, carving, metal-work, posters, making costumes, drama, Christmas decorations, etc.

Meets mainly in subgroups. ☐

EVANGELISM Team is involved in door-to-door distribution of literature, at Christmas and at other times, special events (e.g. gospel concerts), faith-sharing teams and in keeping the church reaching out to people. Meets regularly for training, updates, and prayer. ☐

PRACTICAL Team involves building and maintenance of church structure and equipment, P.A. System, garden, catering, moving furniture, transport, child-minding and practical help for individuals. Meets when necessary for planning and prayer.

☐

Anything else you feel that you could offer? Please outline it below:

....

Please do not tick too many boxes! One main commitment, with one or two lesser ones would be plenty. When filled in please hand to Ryder or Heather.

Name..

Bramingham Park Church.

Appendix 4

TEAM PROFILES

Here are examples of the profiles each team developed after the teams were set up through the questionnaires. These were produced to help people in the church, and those who were to come subsequently to clarify their giftings and help the individual teams to understand their responsibilities in the church.

---

1. ARTS TEAM.

The Arts team is a group of Christian people with artistic talents which they wish to use to glorify Jesus and spread the Gospel.

Arts encompass:

1. Embroidery, tapestry, banner making, costume making.
2. Publicity materials e.g. leaflets, posters.
3. Drama, dance, poetry, Bible reading.
4. Woodwork, Christmas decorations, table decorations, flower arranging.

The AIMS of the Arts Team are:

1. To meet in small groups to pray and seek God's guidance in all that we do.
2. To give visual representation to the Holy Spirit's leading.
3. To give Jesus worship through our artistic creativity.
4. To work closely with all other teams meeting the artistic needs of Bramingham Park Church.

2. EVANGELISM TEAM.

The Evangelism Team is a group of Christians who are eager to share their faith whenever and wherever they can.

They AIM to:
- bring evangelism before the church as its primary task.
- reach as many people as possible of all ages, races, and backgrounds with the good news of Jesus and his love.

- explain it in ways that are relevant to the people concerned.
With the Bible and their own personal story of faith as basic tools, members of the team share their faith, and encourage others to do so, both inside and outside the church building by various means.

For example:
- personal conversations.
- literature distribution.
- gospel concerts.
- social events for children/young people/senior citizens etc.
- street drama.

The team whole heartedly backs those of its number (and others) whom God calls to short or long term missionary work elsewhere.

The team aims to keep the vision of world evangelism alive, and to bring information of what God is doing in other places.

The Evangelism Team works in co-operation with other teams in the ongoing work of the church.

The team meets monthly for prayer and planning.

3. FINANCE TEAM.

'If I am going to help my brother, I must meet three conditions. First, I must have the means necessary to meet his need. Second, I must know that the need exists. Third, I must be loving enough to share...' and further 'You may think that because you have discussed a need, or even prayed about it, that you have done your duty, but love involves more than words - it calls for deeds.'
Warren

The AIMS of the Finance Team are to:

1. Endeavour to prayerfully, thoughtfully, and responsibly give consideration while administering the financial requirements of the church.
2. Keep accurate accounts of all income and expenditure, and make the church aware of our financial situation on a regular basis.
3. Have the books audited at the end of each financial year.
4. Advise the church members of the various means of giving, especially tithing and financial covenants.
5. Allocate all monies sensibly, and in ways that will honour God and bring glory to his name.

6. Meet regularly to discuss and make achievable targets regarding the general running of the church.
7. Humbly seek God's will and purpose in all that we do, especially in our giving.

John 3:16. Ecclesiastes 10:19.

4. PASTORAL TEAM.

The AIM of the Pastoral Team is to:

Serve the family of the church by caring for the needs of the Family, their relatives and friends, and all who come to the fellowship.

The GOAL of the Pastoral team is to:

Achieve a real strengthening of the Family, and to try to meet spiritual and physical needs by the care given.

Some examples of Pastoral Care are:

- To visit/send cards to people who are unwell, bereaved, had new babies, are confined to home, or are in hospital.

- To ensure a welcome is given to all new people who attend any service or meeting, including some form of follow-up, according to their needs and our ability to meet those needs.

- To enable God's Family to confide its problems to us and when people have difficulties in regularly attending services.

- To try to be available to listen and pray, and to be a friend in times of trouble and need.

5. PRACTICAL TEAM.

The Practical Team members seek to use their practical skills in a spiritual way, doing all things cheerfully to the glory of God, and for the benefit of others. They also seek to encourage other people to do the same.

The team is responsible for the church building, its equipment, and the surrounding land, and has a wide range of duties.

Through example, encouragement, and rotas the team tries to involve the whole church family in practical tasks.

The tasks undertaken by a team member will depend on their personal circumstances and abilities.

Everyone is welcome to be involved in this team regardless of age or gender.

The tasks currently undertaken by the practical team include:

1. Building and extending the property. This involves carpentry, tacking, lagging, electrical work, plumbing, painting, artexing etc.

2. Maintenance of, and improvement to, the grounds, gardens, which includes grass cutting, strimming, weeding, planting, fencing, creosoting and painting.
3. Maintenance and improvement of the outside building including painting, cleaning windows, replacing broken panes, replacing slates etc.
4. Maintaining the inside which includes replacing light bulbs, painting, cleaning the toilets, basins, cookers, carpets, windows and furniture. Maintaining and organising the kitchen equipment, checking the electrical and plumbing installations, organising storage and storage areas etc.
5. Providing for the practical needs of others. This includes making tea/coffee, preparing meals, washing dishes, laundry of tea-towels/hand towels, washing tables/work tops, mending Bibles and song books, oiling doors, cleaning furniture, and equipment, providing transport for both people and equipment, cleaning away rubbish, setting up P A and other equipment, chairs and tables for services and other events, producing rotas (and trying to encourage people to read them!).

The team seeks to please the Lord by the quality of its work, its willing cheerful attitude and its friendly service in the name of Christ.

The team believes that God can use these things to help others feel welcome in the Church and to come to faith in Jesus for themselves.

The team believes that there is a 'spiritual gift' for building (Exodus 31:1-5) and that church maintenance is a spiritual ministry (Numbers 1:51). Other Bible references are Matt 10:24; 20:26-28; John 17:14,15; Ephes. 4:12; 1 Cor 15:58.

6. PRAYER CORE.

The Prayer Core is a body of people committed to praying for:
1. The building up of God's church locally and globally for renewal and spiritual growth.
2. To intercede in prayer for known concerns, for the leadership of the church, also for national and international needs.
3. To encourage and motivate each other, and the church, to pray and to share answers to prayer.
4. To 'listen' to God's voice and His will for our church.

Various activities may include:
- days of prayer.
- fasting.
- retreats.
- house groups specifically for prayer.
5. To oversee and follow up prayer chain/wheel requests.
6. To support the minister and family, and leaders in prayer.
7. To promote love and openness with God and each other.

7. PRAYER MINISTRY.

The Prayer Ministry Team is a group of caring men and women committed to the Lord Jesus Christ and seeking to live under the power of His Holy Spirit. They have a God-given gift of ministering His love to all who seek to know and experience Him in their lives, and are trained in Christian counselling.

The Prayer Ministry Team believe that:

- God alone can heal and save through His Son Jesus Christ and by the power of His Holy Spirit, desiring everyone to be set free from sin, guilt, shame, fear and Satan's influence. Luke 9:1-2; John 8:36.

- God's Holy Spirit is with us today to heal people in body, mind, and spirit, using very ordinary people to fulfil His purposes here on earth. Acts 3:6-10; Ephesians 2:10.

- It is both Biblical and practical to pray for, and with, one another in order to open up channels for God's love and healing to pour down on His people. Acts 28:7-9; James 5:14-15.

- God meets us in a very real way at the point of our need.

- This ministry is to bring praise and glory to God. Psalm 96:4; Mark 2:12.

Members of the Prayer Ministry Team AIM to follow and be guided by the Holy Spirit at all times, and to obey His directions when ministering God's love to His people. Romans 8:26-27.

The MODEL we look to and learn from is our Lord Jesus Christ as seen in the Bible. John 14:12.

The Prayer Ministry Team meets regularly for training and prayer.

Anyone who feels a need for prayer or counselling is invited to contact the Team Leader.

8. SECRETARIAL TEAM.

The Secretarial Team AIMS to serve the Church at Bramingham Park in the following ways:

1. To assist in administering the church, its membership and its premises, to enable it to carry out its real work of spreading the Word of God.
2. To assist in reaching out into Bramingham Park, to bring to it the Word of God, and to ensure that it is aware of the life and work of the church.
3. To accurately record events and decisions and assist with ancillary correspondence and other matters arising therefrom and to keep a record of the life and work of the church, whether in written form or recorded on video.
4. To communicate with members of the church by oral or written means, including the publication of a magazine, and running of a library.
5. To communicate with other churches and secular bodies, including (where necessary) representation at meetings, and dealing with correspondence.
6. To assist in complying with legal and social obligations imposed on or accepted by the church in its work and in connection with its premises.

The Secretarial Team therefore seeks to utilise the talents of those who have skills in the written and spoken word and in communicating it, or producing it, by the use of typewriters and other means and those who have organisational and secretarial skills.

It is to be remembered that it is from the work of the early scribes that the Bible has been produced, that Paul's letters recorded the Word of God as revealed to him, and that organisational talents of the early church have led not only to the founding of cathedrals and churches, but early hospices and many charitable institutions.

We seek to contribute to this ongoing work and endeavour to be equal to the challenges facing a new church in a growing new estate.

9. TEACHING TEAM.

The Teaching Team is a group of men and women committed to Christ, with a gift for teaching, who meet every 4-6 weeks to study the Scriptures, pray, discuss and plan the teaching that takes place in the Bramingham Park Church family, and seek to develop the gifts God gives.

The Teaching Team believes;

- that the study and practical application of the Bible is essential to spiritual growth, both individually and as a church.

- that everyone who comes to the church should be provided with an opportunity for life-related Bible study, prayer and friendship during the week, that is appropriate to their age, circumstance and needs.

- that as many as possible should be encouraged to participate in the teaching/learning process.

- that, as Christians, we are all in the process of growth and change, on the way to maturity and wholeness in Christ, and that each teaching event is of equal value.

- that honesty, flexibility and sensitivity to the Lord and to each other are vital principles as we learn together.

Teaching/learning opportunities are provided on Sundays, Mondays, Tuesdays. Wednesdays and Fridays at the moment, although not all are held every week.

The Teaching team AIMS to:

provide a relevant teaching programme that facilitates spiritual, Scriptural growth, so that the whole church family may be equipped to understand and share the Christian Faith.

Its aims are expressed in Ephesians 4:12-16, Colossians 1:9-14, 2 Timothy 2:15-17, and many other Scriptures.

10. WORSHIP TEAM.

The Worship Team is a group of Christian men and women who play a variety of instruments and/or sing.

They meet generally every two weeks to pray, practice, praise and worship in songs, and receive teaching.

The Worship Team believes that:

1. The need to worship is implanted in everyone by God Himself (Is 43:21) and therefore is an essential part of daily life.
2. As we allow ourselves to draw closer to God in worship, He enriches our lives.
3. Praise is our desire to give God the honour that is due to Him. Psalm 86:12.
4. In Spiritual Warfare praise can be a strong weapon (Ps 149:6-9). The more persistent our praise, the more effective our warfare can be.
5. Prayer is an important part of our preparation and practice, as we listen to God and seek His will for us.

6. Honesty, respect, flexibility and sensitivity to the Lord and each other are vital principles as we work together. Praise and Worship opportunities are provided on Sundays, in various weekly meetings, celebrations, and visiting teams to other churches.

The Worship Team AIMS to:
1. Create an atmosphere through worship in which we are able to approach God.
2. Satisfy the basic desire for worship.
3. Minister to others through music and song.
4. Encourage and facilitate children to praise and worship God.
5. Learn new praise and worship songs to teach others.
6. Learn new, and improve on basic techniques, making us more effective on our instruments of worship.
7. Provide Biblical and practical teaching that gives us a fuller insight into the true meaning of praise and worship.

- o O o -

Finally we worked out a Church Profile to explain to anyone wishing to join the Church Family what we were about.

BRAMINGHAM PARK CHURCH.

Our MANDATE is:
To fulfil the prophetic word 'Be My Family. You BE.. and I will BUILD' Matt 16:18.

Our AIM is:
To know Jĕsus Christ and to make him known.

Our VALUES, that help us to decide issues are:
1. The Lordship of Jesus Christ. The Church is His (He died for it, and now lives in it - His people) He is in charge so His will is preeminent.
2. The Bible. We accept the reliability and authority of the Bible, and seek to check everything by this.
3. The Holy Spirit. We believe that He is active, as in the Bible, in power to help, speak, and heal today.
4. The Individual. Each person is of value to the Lord, and to us, no matter what their age, circumstance, race or sex. All can hear from God.
Knowing and doing what He says to us personally is of

primary importance. Individuality must be respected and love be unconditional.

5. People matter more than things. Our priorities are i) sharing the good news that Christ died, is risen and will come again ii) personal growth. Property and programmes are secondary.

Our LIFE is built on:

1. A Commitment:

> To LOVE:
> - the Lord and obey His Word. Mk12:30; Jn 14:15
> - One Another as we are unconditionally. Jn 13:34-35;15:13.
> - Those needing Jesus to bring them to know Him. Mtt 28:19-20.

2. A Covenant:

> WE commit ourselves as the Family of God on Bramingham Park
> to the Lord Jesus and to one another to:
> - Worship and serve the Lord,
> - Teach and obey His Word,
> - Love and serve one another,
> - Make and baptise disciples,
> - And bear witness in the power of the Holy Spirit
> to Christ crucified, risen, and coming again.

3. A Confession:

> 'We individually CONFESS
> Jesus Christ as 'My Lord and my God',
> accept the authority of the Bible,
> and seek to live under the Lordship of Jesus Christ in the power of the Holy Spirit.

Appendix 5

LEADERSHIP MODELS

Here I describe a more typical idea and form of church leadership that tends to be 'pyramidical', and the model that we evolved which could be called 'molecular'. In this appendix I try to contrast and compare their respective strengths and weakness

Pyramid Model

Leader/Pastor/Vicar

Elders

Deacons

Other Officers

Members

Each represents an individual

Although the Leader/pastor, and deacons and elders in most Free Churches are chosen by the main body of members (in Anglicanism there is a different process) the net result is similar i.e. most authority and decision making in practice 'comes down', or is filtered through the 'down process'

Strengths:
- there is more of a finger on the pulse by the leader and more control.
- things can sometimes get done quicker.
- more people can get involved in leadership at different levels.
- leadership appears 'strong'.

Weaknesses:
- the main leader can become aloof, and have too much power.
- when the leader is ill/away/leaves he is replaced by a substitute (church secretary or 'elders' takes control - one of whom is appointed/elected/ or assumes leadership)
- accountability is variable once leadership is established.

- the 'higher up' leaders become the more those leaders can be uninvolved in regular activities apart from decision making.
- often the ordinary members feel distanced, unimportant, and can drift along rather than be active, feeling 'we' do all the work while 'they' pontificate.
- this model of leadership tends to promote a POWER concept of leadership.

Molecular Model

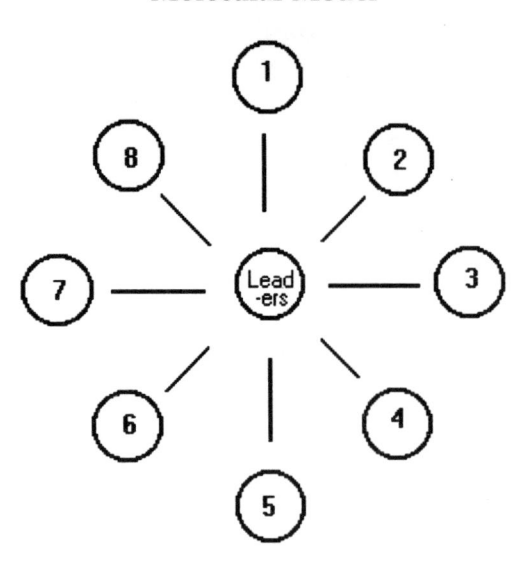

Each circle represents a team - ie worship, pastoral, evangelism, etc. Central circle is where the leaders from each team meet.

Process:
- Each gifting team chooses from its group its own leader who is confirmed later by the whole membership of the church.
- At the centre is a Leadership Team for the leaders of each team to meet for prayer and support.
- The Leadership Team may be overseen by a minister/pastor who is chosen by the total membership, or by one of the leadership team.
- The overall leader, if invited by the church from outside its membership, may be a member of a gifting team but is

responsible primarily for the leaders.
- All gifts and ministries (even 'the minister') are reviewed annually.

Strengths:

- all team leaders have grass roots support because they are chosen by their team, not imposed from outside.
- all team leaders are a working member of their team, not a figurehead.
- all teams, and therefore all team leaders, have equal value in the leadership team.
- unassuming people can become leaders.
- In our set-up any problem had a time limit due to the annual review.
- all members are free to discover and grow gifts and by trial and error find out what are not their gifts and are free to leave a particular team at the end of the year without loss of face.
- all functions in church carry on as normal when the minister is away/sick as the work is team based not leader based.
- all work continues in a team if the team leader is away/sick as work is team based.
- this model of leadership is based on a SERVANT model.

Weaknesses:

- it takes longer to set up.
- is more vulnerable and requires much trust within each team and the whole body.
- good communication with and between each team leader is essential.
- help with Bible input/delegation/talking problems through etc. for each team leader is essential or they will get overwhelmed and try to do all the team work themselves. This is why the overall leader is responsible primarily for the team leaders.
- people can feel isolated within their teams if there are not occasions for general communication - hence the need for our monthly TalkBack for all church members.
- leaders may appear weak because they are unassuming.

An alternative and more detailed diagram of the 'molecular' leadership model:

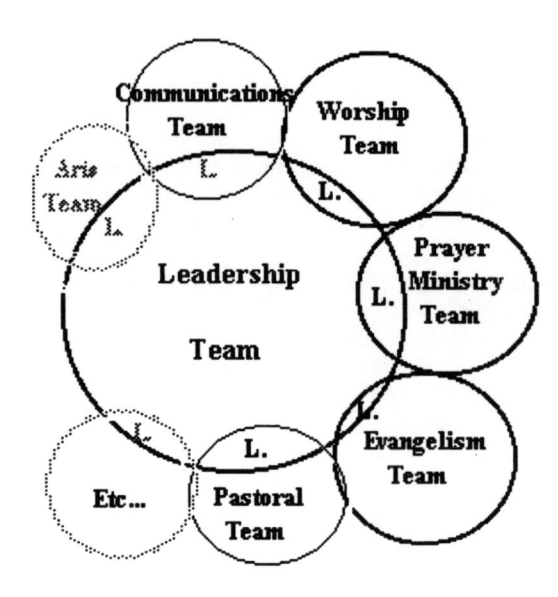

L = A Team Leader

Appendix 6

COUNTDOWN HISTORY
of Bramingham Park Church

1980

    Vision by local Baptist Minister and Church. Consultation with and through local Ecumenical Body with various.
    denominations. Only Baptists interested.

1983

    Vision adopted by Bedfordshire Baptist Association (BBA).
    Consultations with parish church about shared land/property - legal problems. Baptists go it alone. Baptist Home Mission promises ministerial grant

1985

May	Invitation by BBA to Ryder & Heather Rogers to Church Plant.
Aug.	House bought on the estate by BBA.
27	Rogers arrive.
Sept.	Visiting neighbours' homes begins. Christians arrive at house to talk about the church.
Oct.5	Induction to Initial Pastorate at BBA Autumn Assembly.
Oct.6	Invitation to tea of neighbours to discuss church possibilities.
Oct.7	Systematic door to door visiting starts.
Oct.27	Meeting in home for tea and worship. Decision to meet regularly each Sunday afternoon for worship & tea. Prophecy 'Be MY Family. This set the direction for Family Worship. Start studying each Sunday: Principles, Values & practices for being a church
Nov.1	Rainbow Party for children to counteract Halloween - later Rainbow Club.
Dec.6	Monday Night Home Group starts for prayer, Bible study, and fellowship.
Dec.7	Christmas card distribution to every house on the estate.

Dec.24 Christmas Eve Midnight Carol Service in A-frame (Sales Information Office)
Regular Sunday services held at 3.00pm in A-Frame.

1986
Jan.5 First Communion Service.
Jan.7 Neighbourhood Pilot Bible Study Group for Jonah/Malachi.
Mar.20 1st visit of Lou Lewis.
Aug. Home Mission Task Force team arrive, trained for door to door work.
BarBQ for young people etc.
Aug.10 First Blessing Service for a child.
Nov.30 First Baptisms in portable baptistry in A-frame.

1987

Problems with mobility on and off the estate. Pray for a solid nucleus.
Jun.7 Second baptismal service.
Jun.11 Site for church building bought by BBA through Baptist Union for £20,000.
Funds from Bramingham, plus personal gifts, gifts from other churches and BBA help realise £30,000.
Building plans submitted to Luton Borough and later accepted.
Sept.20 First Covenant Service for those committed to Christ, one another and the work we are doing. 21 members sign.
Oct. Constitution evolves with Commitment & Covenant & Values. Attempt to keep it simple.
Nov.8 Third baptismal service.

1988
Feb.28 Talkbacks began on monthly basis for listening to God and planning.
May 25 Building starts with site-stripping.
June Started studying 'Gifts and Ministries' to form 'Gifting Teams'.
July 28 Baptist Union Building Fund approve £50,000 grants.
Jul.10 First Stage Constitution accepted by BBA.
Jul.19 First funeral in A-frame.
Oct. Questionnaires distributed & returned on basis 'every individual is important and gifted.'

Nov.	Within teams members prayerfully look for one person with a leadership gifting. Names to be confirmed by Church Membership at Talkback.

1989

Leadership Team emerges on the basis of Function not Position.

Mar 5	First Leaders Team Meeting.
June	Tools stolen from site shed.
Oct.7	Bramingham Park Church recognised and welcomed into BBA.

1990

Apr.8	March from Sales Information Office into our own property.
	Talkback. Rogers' asked to lead church into the 90's.
Apr.15	First Baptismal Service in our own church building.
Sept.15	First wedding.

1991

Apr.10	John Pantry Evangelistic weekend.
Apr.17	First funeral in church.

1993

Jul.6	Ryder & Heather resign leadership and apply to Baptist Missionary Society to work in Albania. They remain members.

1994

Jan.1	First Missionaries sent out - Ryder & Heather Rogers - to Albania.

Appendix 7

LEAFLET

After many visits by Jehovah's Witnesses we produced the following leaflet, in a format that folds into three, to show a number of things that Christians possess that Jehovah's Witnesses do not have.

Do you have

a 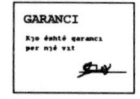 GUARANTEE?

You know if something is genuine if you have a guarantee

These are things that the Lord God has guaranteed

We are guaranteed
1. Eternal Life (1)
2. Forgiveness (2)
3. That we children of God (3)
4. That we will see Jesus personally (4)
5. That we will live with Jesus for ever (5)
6. That we have received the Holy Spirit (6)
7. The power of God (7)
8. That the Lord is with us now (8)
9. That we can the Lord God Jehovah 'My Father' (9)

IF
you are not sure that you have these things -
What should you do?

1. Change or in Bible language 'Repent' (10) because we are all sinners 
2. Believe that Jesus died on the cross as the sacrifice for us (12) and that he rose again (13) to give eternal life (14)
3. Welcome Jesus into your heart as your Lord (15)
4. Receive his Spirit (16)
5. Confess that Jesus is Lord (17)

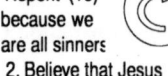

Then you will have

this GUARANTEE

Anything that does not have this guarantee is not genuine

These are things that Jehovah's Witnesses, who say that they are Christians, do not have. In fact they are not Christians if they are truly Jehovah's Witnesses

This name Jehovah gave to his people the Jews (18)

Christians are Jesus Witnesses (19)

Verses in the Bible
1. Ephesians 1v7
2. 1 John 1v9
3. John 1v12
4. 1 John 3v2
5. Acts 2v20; 7v14,15
6. Galatians 4v6; 1 John 4v13
7. Acts 1v8
9. Romans 8v15
10. Acts 17v30
11. Romans 3v23
12. 1 Corinthians 15v3; 1 Peter 2v24
13. Romans 4v25
14. John 14v19
15. Revelation 3v20
16. Acts 2v38; Romans 8v9
17. John 20v38; Romans 8v9
18. Isaiah 43v10
19. Acts 1v8

171

Appendix 8

CHURCH ATTENDANCES

A record was kept of the attendances at Sunday and Midweek meetings.

This is a picture of Sunday attendances when numbers fluctuated dramatically. Any weekly graph looked more like a porcupine and could be quite depressing. Mobility on our estate was dramatic. In our road alone out of 35 house over 66% were sold once, 40% sold twice, and 23% three times (some even four times) during our eight years there.

An annual average Sunday attendance gave us a more realistic and encouraging steadily upward picture.

CHURCH ATTENDANCES
Weekly Averages

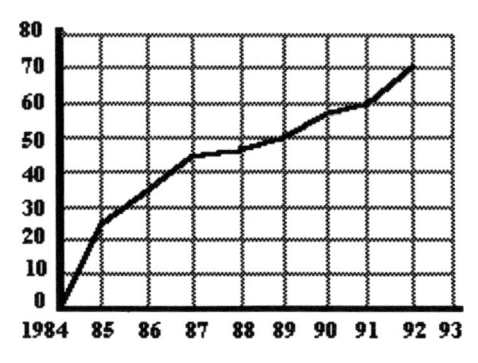

Appendix 9

APOSTOLIC PERSONS AND PEOPLE

My thoughts on this fundamental theme for church planting began when I was studying Church Growth whilst on a Sabbatical at London Bible College in 1982. Slowly a development and adaptation grew in my heart and mind as I looked at the Scriptures and the situation we found ourselves in later as Church planters in the UK and in Albania.

It basically started with Ephesians 4v11-13 and the ideas and diagram of M Harper in his book 'Let My People Grow' about leadership in the local church.

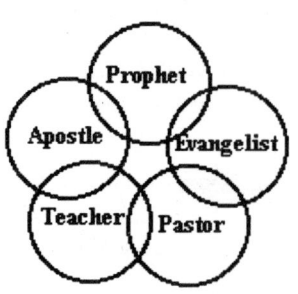

**Leadership Gifts
in the Church
Ephesians 4v11**

As I pondered over the subject of leadership in the church I wondered about the 'Apostolic' Gifting and Ministry, looking at what the Bible said about it, and if, and how, any of this might apply to today.

Whilst agreeing with many of the aspects the Restorationists held to on the subject of Apostles, I couldn't accept the complete package as I questioned a few things they said.

Paul wrote about his apostolic calling in Galatians chs 1,2, and about the 'signs of an apostle' in Romans 15 v18-20. The Bible records, as well as talks about, apostolic ministry in Acts.

From this I came to understand that an apostle is someone who is involved in church planting and is given most, if not all,